✦✦✦✦✦✦✦✦✦✦✦✦✦✦✦✦✦✦

BASEBALL
SUPERSTARS

Lou Gehrig

✦✦✦✦✦✦✦✦✦✦✦✦✦✦✦✦✦✦

Hank Aaron
Ty Cobb
Lou Gehrig
Derek Jeter
Randy Johnson
Mike Piazza
Kirby Puckett
Jackie Robinson
Ichiro Suzuki
Bernie Williams

BASEBALL SUPERSTARS

Lou Gehrig

Ronald A. Reis

CHELSEA HOUSE
PUBLISHERS
An imprint of Infobase Publishing

LOU GEHRIG

Chelsea House
An imprint of Infobase Publishing
132 West 31st Street
New York NY 10001

Library of Congress Cataloging-in-Publication Data
Reis, Ronald A., 1941-
 Lou Gehrig / Ronald A. Reis.
   p. cm. — (Baseball superstars)
 Includes bibliographical references and index.
 ISBN-13: 978-0-7910-9423-5
 ISBN-10: 0-7910-9423-5
 1. Gehrig, Lou, 1903-1941—Juvenile literature. 2. Baseball players—United States—
Biography—Juvenile literature. I. Title. II. Series.
 GV865.G4R47 2007
 796.357092—dc22   2007006209

Series design by Erik Lindstrom
Cover design by Ben Peterson and Joo Young An

Printed in the United States of America

Bang EJB 10 9 8 7 6 5 4 3 2 1

This book is printed on acid-free paper.

✫✫✫✫✫✫✫✫✫✫✫✫✫✫✫✫✫✫

CONTENTS

1

Grand Slam

Wrigley Field was not yet Wrigley Field on June 26, 1920, the day Lou Gehrig stood awestruck within the 18,000-seat major-league ballpark. Cubs Park it was called, home of the National League's Chicago Cubs.

No matter the name, surely 17-year-old Lou must have wondered how he had come so far, so soon.

At almost six feet tall and 180 pounds, Lou, a senior, was here with his teammates from New York City's High School of Commerce to play against Chicago's Lane Tech High School. The nation's unofficial inter-city high school baseball championship was on the line. Just one game would be held. More than 8,000 fans had massed at Grand Central Terminal in Manhattan to see the lads off. And 2,000 were there to hail the team as its train, puffing and steaming, pulled into "Wild and Woolly" Chicago.

Much was expected of Lou, for he had left New York with a reputation as one awesome slugger. Indeed, the *Chicago Tribune* warned its readers the day before the big game, "The Gotham boys have a first baseman, Louis Gehrig, who is called the 'Babe Ruth' of the high schools. If he gets hold of one, it is quite likely to be driven over the right wall at the Cubs' park."

Come game time, with 6,000 fans in the stands, an unheard-of number for a high school ball game, electricity sparked the air. Yet, by the ninth inning, the crowd had not seen much of "the Babe" in Lou.

The first inning, Lou fouled off two pitches and then took a walk.

In the second inning, he grounded back to the pitcher.

In the fourth, he struck out with a man on base.

And in the sixth inning, heavy hitter Lou, from big city New York, walked again.

True, with but an inning to go, Commerce led, 8-6. It's just that "Steady Lou," as he would come to be called, had not had much to do with the team's success—so far.

At the start of the ninth inning, Lane Tech's desperation showed on every player's face. They had but one chance to retire Commerce and stage a rally in the bottom of the inning to overcome the two-run deficit.

As the top of the inning painfully progressed, Lane's new pitcher, right-hander Norris Ryrholm, eventually forced two outs on Commerce. That was the good news. The bad news for Chicago was that, as Lou stepped to the plate, probably for his last time at bat, three men were on base.

A long ball now from Commerce's crack hitter would be more than just a home run—it would be a grand slam. Lane Tech's hopes for a comeback would all but evaporate.

Lou, batting lefty, eased into the batter's box, his left foot closer to the plate than his right, and stared out at Norris. He let the first pitch go by without swinging. Then Norris delivered what he thought would be a dynamite backdoor slider. Lou squeezed the bat and swung vigorously, snapping his wrists at the last possible moment.

Whack! The ball vaulted upward, soaring higher and higher, over the park's right-field brick wall and out of sight. Witnesses say it bounced once on Sheffield Avenue, coming to rest on the wooden porch of a small house facing the ballpark.

Final score: Commerce 12, Lane Tech 6. Lou's dream was a reality; he had smashed one clear out of a major-league park. "Babe Gehrig" was on his way.

ONE TO SURVIVE

As the "Gay 1890s" rolled over into the twentieth century, the times were changing. During the first few years of the 1900s, the world, and especially the United States, seemed rushing toward a dazzling, unimagined future.

On December 14, 1903, Wilbur and Orville Wright flipped a coin. Wilbur won, and thus made the initial attempt to fly their 4-cylinder, 12-horsepower flying machine. It stalled. Three days later, at 10:35 A.M., 32-year-old Orville took his turn, ushering in the age of flight by staying aloft for 12 seconds on a wind-swept beach in North Carolina.

In the same year, Henry Ford founded the Ford Motor Company, claiming, "I will build a car for the great multitude." In 1908, the first Model T rolled off his assembly line. Nearly 15.5 million would eventually be sold in the United States alone.

At the intersection of Broadway and Fifth Avenue, in New York City, a new kind of building stretched to completion in 1902—20 stories high. Called the Flatiron Building, because its shape resembled an old-style clothes iron, it was considered the nation's first true skyscraper.

New York, or more precisely, New Yorkers, were rushing uptown, too. With completion of the nation's first subway near

New York City's Flatiron Building, completed in 1902, was considered to be the first true skyscraper. During those early years of the twentieth century, the nation seemed to be hurtling into the future—Henry Ford began his automobile company, and the Wright brothers flew the first airplane. That idea of a bright future lured hundreds of thousands of immigrants to the United States—immigrants like Heinrich and Christina Gehrig, whose son, Lou, was born in 1903.

at hand, commuters would no longer have to fight through crowded and filthy streets to get off Manhattan Island and travel north into the Bronx.

And folks would eventually come to the Bronx. For 1903 was the year that the New York Highlanders ball club started play, first perching themselves on the highest point in Manhattan, giving rise to their name. By the time the team built its own ballpark, a true stadium, 20 years later in the Bronx, the Highlanders had become the mighty Yankees.

It was also in New York in 1903 that a future Yankee, and not just any Yankee, came kicking and screaming into the world. On June 19, 14-pound Henry Louis Gehrig became the son of poor, struggling, immigrant parents from Germany, Christina and Heinrich Gehrig. Lou would be the only one of their four children to survive past infancy.

ALL WORK AND PLENTY OF PLAY

Lou's father immigrated to the United States in 1888, his mother, in 1899. The two met, fell in love, and married in 1900, in New York City.

Both parents had been part of the multitude of Europeans who were venturing to the United States in the last decades of the nineteenth century. Part, to be sure, of the "tired, [the] poor, [the] huddled masses yearning to breathe free," as proclaimed at the base of that welcoming colossus, the Statue of Liberty. Soon after their marriage, Christina and Heinrich found lodging in the lower-middle-class section of Yorkville in Manhattan.

Heinrich Gehrig had skills that his new country needed, a trade that would enable him to work. "Pop," as he liked to be called, was an art-metal mechanic. Unfortunately, Heinrich also had personality traits that often kept him out of work. He liked his beer and his gambling.

Furthermore, Heinrich was frequently ill, further diminishing his employment prospects. Curiously, Lou would come to be known as the Iron Horse for never missing a day on the job in his 14 years as a Yankee ballplayer.

Mother Gehrig was another matter. At more than 200 pounds (91 kilograms), Christina was a robust worker who took in cleaning and did the cooking for her neighbors. She developed a reputation as an excellent baker. She put young Lou to work, too, delivering laundry and picking up supplies.

★ ★ ★ ★ ★ ☆

THE IMMIGRANT EXPERIENCE

If the Statue of Liberty was the beacon, Ellis Island was the portal through which they came. The two together, each on its own plot of land in New York Harbor, signaled hope to all who would come. Hope for freedom and for economic opportunity.

From the last decades of the nineteenth century till after the Great Depression of the 1930s, they arrived by the millions, mostly from Europe, to seek a better life. From 1892, the year Ellis Island officially opened, to 1954, more than 12 million immigrants came through its doors. Today, 4 out of 10 Americans can trace their heritage via Ellis Island.

The Statue of Liberty, a gift from France, was carted to the United States in 350 individual pieces and then assembled on "Bedloe's Island" in 1886. Engraved on a bronze plaque at the statue's base are American poet Emma Lazarus's famous lines:

Give me your tired, your poor,
Your huddled masses yearning to breathe free,
The wretched refuse of your teeming shore.
Send these, the homeless, tempest-tost to me,
I lift my lamp beside the golden door!

Tost, indeed! Although some immigrants could afford the luxury accommodations of the day—sailing first or second

For his efforts, Lou received trolley fare and, on one memorable occasion, with money "borrowed" from dad's gambling stash, a visit to Coney Island. Young Lou rode the roller coaster and ate all the hot dogs and ice cream he wanted.

Christina saw to it that, as poor as the family was, Lou always had plenty to eat. As a result, "little" Lou soon became even bigger Lou. As he got older, Lou's body grew exceptionally

✮ ✮ ✮ ✮ ✮ ✮

class—most, by far, made the trip below deck, in what was called steerage. The quarters were, in the words of Charles Dickens, "an appalling little world of poverty." In the early decades of the immigrant rush, it was not uncommon for up to 30 percent of those attempting the voyage to fall victim to starvation and disease before the two- to three-month journey ended.

Still, they came. If they were lucky enough to pass inspection on Ellis Island (where immigrants were examined for contagious diseases, like scarlet fever and diphtheria), only then could their new life begin.

Some became famous. Future football coach Knute Rockne, of Notre Dame, arrived in 1893 from Norway. Actor, singer, and songwriter Al Jolson came from Lithuania in 1894. Samuel Goldwyn, the man who would produce the movie *The Pride of the Yankees* in 1942, made it to America in 1896. And, one of the most famous arrivals of all, Bob Hope, stepped onto American soil as a 5-year-old lad in 1908.

Others would arrive nearly destitute but would eventually give birth to the famous and noteworthy. Heinrich Gehrig appeared in 1888; Christina Fack, in 1899. They would marry, and in 1903, Christina gave birth to a boy who would go on to became one of the most renowned athletes in all of sports—Lou Gehrig.

strong. Heinrich saw to it that Lou's muscles stood out, often taking the boy to the local gymnasium to pump iron. Pop Gehrig encouraged his son to play sports. For Christmas, he bought Lou a catcher's mitt. Unfortunately, it was for a right-hander. Lou was left-handed. Heinrich knew so little about baseball, he had no idea it would make any difference.

His father's occasional indulgences aside, young Lou grew ever closer to his mother. "He's the only big egg I have in my basket," she was to have said, as reported in Ray Robinson's *Iron Horse: Lou Gehrig in His Time.* "He's the only one of four who lived, so I want him to have the best."

In 1908, the Gehrigs were able to move up a bit, to Washington Heights, on the northern tip of Manhattan. Lou attended Public School 132. Being poor, shy, and in many ways unsure of himself, he received his share of taunting from classmates. Yet, with Lou's growing strength, he was assured of a more or less fight-free grammar-school experience.

Besides, Lou had his sports, and with them, a measure of social acceptance. Although baseball was his favorite pastime, Lou could handle himself quite nicely at various street games, such as marbles, soccer, basketball, and football. Through it all, his studies, his work, and his play, Lou never missed a day of school. As he turned 14, in 1917, Lou graduated from P.S. 132 with perfect attendance.

THE COMMERCE KID

In the fall of 1917, Lou Gehrig did something few in his economic circumstances could or would do—he went on to high school. Most 14-year-olds in these years headed directly to work, on the farms, in the family store, or, on occasion, in the bustling urban factories, satisfied with their grammar-school education.

Not Lou, and certainly not Lou's mother. Christina wanted her son to become an architect or an engineer, to have a profession. So, off to New York's High School of Commerce

Lou Gehrig and his mother, Christina, visited the Yankees' training quarters in St. Petersburg, Florida, in March 1931. When Lou was a child, Christina Gehrig took in cleaning and cooked for neighbors to earn money for the family. She also made sure that her son received an education. As for baseball, early on, she was not a fan—at least as far as her son playing the sport. To her, it was "a game for bummers."

she sent her Lou, a long ride on the elevated trains to 155 West 65th Street.

Commerce was pretty much defined by its name: an all-boys school that taught the fundamentals of bookkeeping, typing, and clerical work. Few of its students actually went on to college.

Lou arrived at Commerce each day, dressed not to impress; he could little afford to do so. His clothes were the usual pass-arounds, minus an overcoat. Even on the coldest days, in the dead of winter, Lou came to school without a coat. His family simply had no money to buy him one.

Lou's schoolwork was passable, but it was in athletics that he began to excel. Curiously, in the beginning, baseball was the sport in which he stood out the least. In the field, Lou was just plain clumsy. Yet, his coach, Harry Kane, kept working with him. Lou practiced, practiced, and then practiced some more. The kid, though, was not born to play the game. "Some ball-players have natural-born ability," Lou later said, as recounted in Jonathan Eig's biography, *Luckiest Man: The Life and Death of Lou Gehrig.* "I wasn't one of them." With his fellow players hitting him grounders and fly balls over and over again, Lou did get better—a lot better.

Yet, it was not in the outfield, or even at first base, that the sprouting Lou made an impression. It was when he entered the batter's box. By his junior year, Lou had developed into one of the most powerful hitters in high school baseball.

Lou still worked, earning money while studying and playing sports. One day he showed up to football practice, his face all covered in soot. It turns out, Lou had had to take over for his ill father, who was working as a janitor.

As Lou entered his senior year, he had not made many friends. Girls were never seen in his company. When not playing sports, Lou was content to be by himself. Yet, Lou's growing physical stature and dogged practice allowed him to stand out on any field of play. In baseball, under Commerce's capable coach, the high school had assembled an impressive team. Lou was a key factor in its success.

GAME FOR BUMMERS

Baseball in the pre-Babe Ruth era, before the Roaring '20s thundered in, was not the game it would become later, when Lou played professionally. It was a time of ballparks and fields, not stadiums. Players wore heavy wool uniforms with no names or numbers. It was the Dead Ball Era, when, by the ninth inning, the balls were often lopsided and soggy, all but precluding home runs. (One ball was often used for 100 pitches or more.) Baseball was a pitching-dominated, defensive game, mainly one of wits and speed. Few players made a habit of swinging for the fences.

Baseball's homespun characteristics failed to prevent scandal from intruding, however. The year before Lou graduated from Commerce, in 1920, eight players on the Chicago White Sox, including "Say it ain't so" Joe Jackson, were accused of fixing the 1919 World Series. Though never convicted of any crime, all eight were expelled from baseball for life.

The game, though, remained the national pastime. So much so that high school baseball had become a big deal. In 1920, the *Daily News* in New York sponsored a game between two top high school teams, one from New York and one from Chicago. Commerce High School got the nod from the East; Lane Tech would represent the city out West.

Though Lou was a shoo-in to make the trip, he first had to get his mother's permission.

"No!" was Christina's initial answer, when Lou asked, as related in *Luckiest Man.* "This baseball is a waste of time. It will never get you anywhere."

Lou pleaded, "I want to go, Mom. All the other boys are going."

Mother kept insisting, "Baseball was a bunch of nonsense, a game for bummers." She felt it would only take Lou away from his studies.

When Lou agreed to attend college after graduation, Christina's resolve began to soften—ever so slightly. Then, with a timely intervention from coach Kane, who promised to take full responsibility for Lou on the four-day trip, his mother relented.

With Lou's return from Chicago, cheers of his grand slam still ringing in his ears, New York went wild. Five thousand screaming New Yorkers greeted the *Twentieth Century Limited*, as the train, with the high-spirited team, pulled into Grand Central Terminal. The next day, Lou's photograph appeared in the *Daily News*.

Christina still was not convinced that baseball was anything but a trivial pastime. Nonetheless, she clipped out the article, with its headline, "Louis Gehrig Hits Ninth-Inning Homer With Bases Loaded," and hid it away in a drawer.

2

Columbia Lou

Having promised Mom that he would attend college after graduation, Lou Gehrig began to search for an institution of higher learning that offered sports. He did not have far to look.

Columbia University, on New York's Upper West Side, may not have been a baseball or football powerhouse, but it was, nonetheless, a prestigious, private university that took in graduates from the city's upper crust. Would Lou, poor, naive, and socially awkward, fit in at Columbia? Would the snooty student body accept him?

Before he could fret over such issues, Gehrig had two obstacles to overcome. Upon graduation from Commerce, on January 27, 1921, young Lou lacked the credits necessary to enter Columbia. Thus, in February, he enrolled in Columbia's extension program to complete courses in elementary algebra, general chemistry, intermediate German, and literature and composition.

After several months of intensive study, Gehrig finished his courses and passed the College Board examinations. That was one hurdle surmounted. Money, however, to pay tuition and cover expenses, loomed as an ever-present stumbling block. Clearly, Gehrig would need a scholarship. Although the coaches at Columbia were well aware of his exploits on the baseball field, the now six-foot-tall 200-pound athlete with "thighs as big around as a bull's stomach" would enter Columbia on a football scholarship.

GIANTS BRUSH-OFF

Though Gehrig would not officially begin at Columbia until the fall, he did not wait until the leaves fell before swinging a bat for the university. As soon as spring weather warmed the sparse grasses of New York City, Gehrig took to practicing with Columbia's baseball team.

On April 5, wearing a gray sweatshirt, rather than a proper baseball uniform, Gehrig stepped to the plate for Columbia in a game against the Hartford Senators, a minor-league team from the Class A Eastern League. He smashed two home runs. The next day, the *Hartford Times* could not restrain itself in narrating the second slammer—it "went sailing out over the enclosure past a big sundial and almost into the School of Mines. It was a mighty clout and almost worthy of Babe Ruth's best handiwork."

Once again, with that pairing of Gehrig and Ruth in print, major-league scouts renewed their interest in Gehrig. Chief among the spotters was Art Devlin, trolling for the one and only New York Giants.

Devlin made it clear that he spoke for the legendary John McGraw, the Giants' stumpy, feisty manager. If Gehrig would just come by the Giants' ballpark, the Polo Grounds, and attend a tryout, Devlin would see to it that McGraw took a serious look at him.

Hopeful that something might come of it, and in need of money, Gehrig agreed to show up. He dragged his beat-up first baseman's glove into the U-shaped field of the Polo Grounds. Gehrig felt elated to be there, to be auditioning for a team like the Giants. McGraw, it would turn out, could not have cared less.

The tryout got off to a good start. Gehrig belted a half-dozen pitches into the stands. But when the 17-year-old took a stance at first base, he clumsily let a ground ball snake through his legs. McGraw, who had barely noticed the freshman-to-be from Columbia, had, with this one mistake, seen all he needed. "Get this fellow out of here!" he yelled, as described in *Iron Horse*. "I've got enough lousy players without another one showing up."

McGraw's spurning of Gehrig on that cloudy spring day was, it turned out, a monumental management error. He had let the man who would become the greatest first baseman of all time slip past him as surely as that grounder slithered between Gehrig's legs.

Though McGraw forever dismissed the incident, Gehrig never forgot the manager's rejection. "I have often thought," Gehrig said, as quoted in *Luckiest Man*, "because of later developments, if he had given me a real opportunity to make good and taken pains with me, the baseball situation in New York perhaps would have been a lot different in the years that were to come."

HARTFORD MISTAKE

In the 1920s, as today, being an amateur athlete meant one thing. Being a professional athlete meant something more. It wasn't just that, as a rule, professional ballplayers were better than amateurs; professionals got paid for playing.

Amateur athletics, the kind that took place in school, had their own rules and regulations. Most important, student-athletes were forbidden to play for money, to play for pay. If a kid did earn money at a sport, even if only in one game and for pocket change, under regulations in force going back to the late nineteenth century, the youngster could be barred from future participation. He could lose his amateur status and never play college ball again.

In the summer of 1921, Lou Gehrig did something that brought him perilously close to losing the right to engage in any sport for Columbia University—even before he officially became a student.

When Lou was at Commerce High, he took opportunities, from time to time, to earn a buck playing a little baseball. There were plenty of semipro teams around Manhattan. As Eleanor, his future wife, would explain years later in her autobiography, *My Luke and I,* "They'd play on Sunday against teams from other New York neighborhoods or from New Jersey: $35 guaranteed to each team, with $5 for the pitcher. So Lou Gehrig became a pitcher."

These little $5 payoffs were not what would get Gehrig in hot water. After the Giants' rejection, Devlin persuaded the young hitter that it would be perfectly all right for him to spend the summer playing for the Hartford Senators, with whom the Giants had a relationship. Gehrig could earn money, gain experience, and quite possibly the Giants would take another look at him. Hungry for all three possibilities, Gehrig jumped at the chance.

The Giants saw nothing of Gehrig that summer, but others did. Playing under the false name of Lou Lewis, Gehrig wound up in a dozen games for Hartford. He batted .261 in 46 times at bat, going hitless in only three games.

Soon the local papers began to compare this "Lewis" with Ruth, a dead giveaway. Columbia's baseball coach, Andy

Lou Gehrig *(above)* was able to attend Columbia University on a football scholarship. Before he entered the university in 1921, though, he played 12 games of professional baseball with the Hartford Senators—a move that could have ended his college career before it began. When Columbia officials found out, Gehrig was banned from playing football or baseball during his freshman year.

Coakley, promptly visited Gehrig, and the chastened lad quickly returned home to New York.

Gehrig, who surely must have known he was doing something off the mark when he changed his name, was potentially in deep trouble. As a price for his indiscretion, Gehrig was barred from playing any sport at Columbia during his freshman year. He would be allowed to return to football and baseball competition in 1922 and 1923. Since freshmen were not eligible for varsity play anyway, Gehrig got off easy.

OFF AND ON THE FIELD

As Gehrig entered into university life in the fall of 1921, outwardly he appeared to be the "big man on campus." He looked like a youngster bound to succeed: socially, athletically, and even scholastically. Looks, though, could be deceiving.

True, Gehrig was tall and handsome, with bright blue eyes. And he was muscular. If some students found Gehrig reserved and of few words, others could be excused if they saw the strong, silent type in the man.

Gehrig joined a fraternity, Phi Delta Theta. Yet, he rarely hung around with his fraternity brothers. Basically, he waited on their tables and performed other menial tasks.

Shyness and social awkwardness aside, Gehrig's inability to make friends and be part of the "in crowd" rested equally on his lowly economic status. While many of his privileged classmates wore starched shirts and ties, Gehrig "sported" baggy pants and a wrinkled shirt. It was not that he was a slob; he was poor.

Gehrig, it appears, never went out on dates. It seems that, handsome as he was, girls could not afford to be seen with a boy who lacked even decent clothes.

All this rejection cut deep, wounding Gehrig in ways he would not soon forget. He would tell his wife years later of the arrogant mean-spiritedness that his classmates displayed toward him. When Gehrig reached unbelievable stardom as a baseball player, these same classmates would often claim

Lou Gehrig took a swing during a game in 1923 at Columbia University. His play during his first season with Columbia again stirred the interest of baseball scouts—including representatives from the New York Yankees.

Gehrig as one of their own. With few exceptions, he chose not to acknowledge their assertions.

On the field, however, Gehrig was, indeed, "the man." Although he played football for Columbia, fulfilling his scholarship obligations, it was in baseball that Gehrig excelled.

There was the famous sundial incident. Ray Robinson, writing in *Iron Horse*, recounts what a Gehrig teammate, John Donaldson, saw one day: "I was sitting one afternoon, cramming for an exam in Hartley Hall, when I heard a bunch of students down below give a big yell. I looked out the window just in time to see a ball bouncing off the top of the sundial, maybe some four hundred fifty feet from home plate. And there was Lou standing there, in his baggy knickers, grinning from ear to ear."

Then, there was the day the brand-new Yankee Stadium opened up, April 18, 1923. Ruth was there to inaugurate the ballpark with a home run. Gehrig was not. He was busy back on Columbia's South Field awing his own fans. Playing Williams College, Gehrig, as pitcher, struck out 17 batters, walked four, and hit one. At bat, he hit a single and a double and drove in one run. Too bad it was the only run. The Columbia Lions lost, 5-1.

★ ★ ★ ★ ★ ☆

A WHOLE NEW BALL GAME

If there is, today, some dispute as to whether George Herman Ruth, the Sultan of Swat, was the greatest baseball player who ever lived, there is little doubt that he was the most flamboyant. With his play on the field, and his antics off, the Babe garnered headlines across the country and around the world, particularly in Japan. Babe Ruth was a phenomenon. When the "Goliath of the Grand Slam" began to hit those long balls, he changed the game of baseball forever.

In the Dead Ball Era, before the arrival of a harder ball and Babe Ruth, home runs were rare. Most batters did not even swing for them, preferring to choke up on the bat and push, poke, or jab at the pitch. They tried to hit the ball into a hole between defensive players. When the "King of Clout" began going for the fences with every swing, it became, well, a whole new ball game. More batters became full swingers rather than place hitters.

In 1921, this "Prince of Pounders" hit a phenomenal 59 home runs, more than all the other teams in the American League,

As it turned out, 1923 was a good year for Gehrig. The university's powerhouse hitter batted .444, with an amazing slugging percentage of .937. His stats included six doubles, two triples, seven home runs, and five stolen bases. Major-league scouts began to circle once again.

AN OFFER HARD TO RESIST

Chief among the prowlers was Paul Krichell, looking out for Yankee interests. "I think I saw another Ruth today," he told Edward Barrow, the Yankees' general manager, as recalled in *Iron*

★ ☆ ★ ☆ ★

except two. One sportswriter, as noted in Robert Burleigh's book *Home Run* described a king-size carom like this:

"The ball went over the fence, over the street, over the roof-top of another house, atop still another house, and then bounced off down the street two blocks away!"

Fans loved it and kept paying to see more.

It did not take opposing pitchers long to figure out that it was often better to walk the Babe than to let him swing. In 1923, the year Lou Gehrig signed with the Yankees, Ruth received 170 free passes, setting a major-league record. If you include all the walks awarded Ruth, his on-base percentage was over .500. In other words, when Ruth came to the plate, he moved on to first base every other time. No wonder the Yankees, indeed, all teams in the majors, were looking for future Babes, on high school and college campuses, in the minor leagues, and everywhere else. Though the Yankees could not be sure of it at the time, in 1923 they found such a player in Lou Gehrig.

Horse. It was the spring of 1923, and Gehrig, in a game against New York University, had hit yet another ball out of South Field, striking the steps of the library across 116th Street.

The Yankees, in the 20 years since their arrival on the hilltop, had come a long way from their fumbling, scattered beginnings. By 1919, they were ready to take the next step—claim the pennant, maybe even a World Series win. To make that dream, that hunger, a reality, they would, the reasoning went, need a major slugger, a player who could not only generate runs, but bring in the paying fans eager to see the long ball sailing over fences or into outfield stands. They found their man in Babe Ruth. The Yankees bought the future "Sultan of Swat" from the Boston Red Sox.

With the Yanks heading for their third-straight American League pennant in 1923, led by Ruth's home runs, they seemed to have all they needed in their lineup. Nonetheless, thinking ahead, Krichell persuaded Gehrig to show up at Barrow's new Yankee Stadium office to "talk a deal."

The offer came immediately. To acquire Gehrig, the Yankees dangled a contract of $400 per month, or $1,200 for the remainder of the 1923 season—plus a $1,500 signing bonus.

Gehrig was stunned. It was an incredible figure, particularly considering his family's dire economic straits. Gehrig had continued to work at odd jobs as a college student, but there still never seemed to be enough money. Furthermore, Gehrig's mother and father had taken ill—Christina, seriously. Neither was capable of bringing home a dime.

The deciding factor for Gehrig, though, may have been his lack of academic achievement at Columbia. True, he was passing his classes. Yet, as an engineering major, Gehrig was an uninspired student. He wanted to wield a bat, not finger a slide rule. Quitting school would upset his mother, for sure. But the chance to enable his parents to retire from a life of toil—forever—and get paid to play, for the Yankees no less, was a tantalizing inducement.

Still, before putting pen to paper, Gehrig sought advice from a professor, Archibald Stocker. After hearing Gehrig make his case, the teacher leaned back in his chair, and, according to Ray Robinson in *Iron Horse*, said, "Lou, you've been in my class for almost a year. . . . I think you better play ball."

On April 30, 1923, 19-year-old Lou Gehrig signed a contract with the Yankees, the only major-league team for which he would ever play. His parents would never work another day in their lives.

From the Majors
to the Minors

In 1923, the year Lou Gehrig signed with the Yankees, the United States was in recovery. Some would say, full recovery.

Folks were partying everywhere, with dance marathons being the latest Roaring '20s rage. "Joe College," "blind date," "upchuck," and "the real McCoy" were the "in" Jazz Age slang. Silent film star Harold Lloyd thrilled audiences with humorous stunts atop a 12-story skyscraper in his 1923 film, *Safety Last.* All this fun occurred despite, or because of, Prohibition, speak-easies, and bootleg whiskey.

It was a time of joy and escape for a people who had experienced little of either just a few years before.

The Great War, fought from 1914 to 1918, devastated an entire generation. Known as "The War to End all Wars," it became a senseless slaughter, in which at least 15 million people died in Europe, to "make the world safe for democracy," as President Woodrow Wilson famously proclaimed.

In 1918 and 1919, more than 50 million people succumbed to a worldwide influenza pandemic. In the United States, 675,000 perished from the killer virus.

And, just when the misfortune had seemingly come to an end, and citizens could seek recuperation in their favorite pastime, baseball, newspaper headlines proclaimed the 1919 fix of the World Series and the attempted cover-up. "The most gigantic sports swindle in the history of America," as described in Eliot Asinof's *Eight Men Out: The Black Sox and the 1919 World Series*. Soon enough, the White Sox became the Black Sox, and America's loss of innocence seemed complete.

From this dark episode, though, baseball not only recovered, it flourished. With city dwellers wholeheartedly taking to the sport, with cavernous stadiums being built, and with the Babe hitting home runs, Americans, by 1923, had re-embraced their pastime with unparalleled enthusiasm. Lou Gehrig, it would seem, had broken into the majors at just the right time.

ARRIVAL DAY

Being signed by the Yankees did not mean Gehrig would actually be playing for the Yankees, that he would be out there fielding fly balls and swinging a bat with the likes of Bob Meusel, Whitey Witt, Everett Scott, and Babe Ruth. First, Gehrig would have to make the team's roster; then, even more daunting, the starting lineup. For 19-year-old Lou Gehrig, arriving at Yankee Stadium for the first time on June 11, 1923, there was little assurance that either would happen right away.

Still, Gehrig came, on a clear, blue-sky day, eager to impress. He arrived via subway, having paid his nickel fare. Wrapped up in an old newspaper were his spikes and his worn glove. Miller Huggins, the 135-pound (61-kilogram) Yankee manager, was there to greet Gehrig.

Huggins had been hoping that the team was gaining not only a great baseball prospect, but a Jewish one at that. For years, Yankee management had been looking for a Jewish player who, by virtue of his religion, would appeal to the sizable Jewish community in New York. No such luck here. Though "Gehrig" may have sounded Jewish to Huggins and a few others, Gehrig was Lutheran.

As Gehrig and Huggins headed to the clubhouse, they picked up Doc Woods, the team's trainer, along the way. The three approached the Sultan of Swat. "Babe, I want you to meet Lou Gehrig, from Columbia," Woods said, as reported in *Iron Horse*. "Hiya, keed," was Ruth's only response.

Down on the field, Huggins told Gehrig to get a bat. After grabbing the nearest "Louisville Slugger," Gehrig made it to the batter's box. When he rotated the 48-ounce (1.3-kilogram) bat into position, he noticed a name printed squarely on the large barrel: "George 'Babe' Ruth." Gehrig was about to take his first "show-off" batting practice for the potent Yankees, with his idol's bat in hand.

After a few hesitant swings—maybe Gehrig did not want to crack the Babe's stick—the new kid began to wield it in earnest. Jonathan Eig, in *Luckiest Man*, sums up what happened next:

> Huggins, Ruth, and others watched as Gehrig stepped into each pitch, his hips, torso, and shoulders rotating in a compact motion, weight shifting from left foot to right. Shots started clanging off the seats into the right-field bleachers. They were different from the long drives Babe Ruth usually hit. Ruth's homers were moon shots. Gehrig's were bullets.

About Gehrig's first appearance with the Yankees that June day, Waite Hoyt, the team's best pitcher, recalled, in *Luckiest Man*: "We all knew that he was a big-league ballplayer in the making. Nobody could miss him."

Babe Ruth *(right)* discussed the finer points of hitting on June 16, 1923, with his new teammate Lou Gehrig. Gehrig had joined the New York Yankees five days earlier. On his first day, during batting practice, Gehrig cracked ball after ball into the right-field bleachers.

ON THE BENCH

Although another Yankee observed (of Gehrig's performance that first day) that the Babe now knew he had company, Ruth certainly was not worried he would be overshadowed anytime soon. Gehrig may have been on the payroll, but he was not on the team.

To begin with, there was no place for him. Wally Pipp, who had started with the ball club back in 1915, was doing a reasonable job at first base. True, he was not a great hitter, rarely launching balls over the fences. Pipp, though, was only 30 years old in 1923, and the previous year he hit .329, with 90 runs batted in and 9 home runs. His position on the team was secure, at least for the current season when, even as early as mid-June, the Yankees seemed headed for another pennant win.

Besides, Gehrig was a greenhorn. He was inexperienced. On offense, there were those who saw a future Babe. In the field, though, he had yet to develop. Gehrig, too, was naive to the ways of the big leagues. As Niven Busch, writing in *The New Yorker*, said at the time, "Gehrig was one of the most bewildered recruits anyone had ever seen."

Yet, Huggins wanted to keep his new apprentice around, at Yankee Stadium. He wanted Gehrig to soak up all he could about big-league ball. Huggins wanted to whet Gehrig's appetite.

So, over the coming days, Gehrig sat on the bench, watching, thinking, and taking it all in. He invited his mother and father out to see how their boy was earning the "Yankee dollar."

"Did you ever hear the story of the first time Pop and Mom came to see me play at the Stadium?" Gehrig once asked a journalist, as recounted in Eig's *Luckiest Man*. He continued:

> Neither had ever been to a ball game before. I forgot to
> tell them to come early [for batting practice], as there was
> nothing for me to do after the regulars took their positions.

. . . They saw a lot of ballplayers running around, but not their Louie. When I came home for dinner, they asked me, "Well, where were you?" I had to reply, "I was sitting on the bench." "What kind of bummer's game is that where they pay a young man good money to sit on a bench?" stormed my father.

Still, Gehrig did play—somewhat. On June 15, he filled in for Pipp in the ninth inning of a game against the St. Louis Browns. It was his first major-league appearance. On June 18, Gehrig got his chance at bat, in a game against the Detroit Tigers. He struck out.

On August 1, Huggins decided that Gehrig needed some hardening in the minors. The manager sent him back, so to speak, to the Hartford Senators, where Gehrig had had a summer "exposure" two years earlier.

MINOR-LEAGUE SEASONING

Gehrig's mother had yet to accept her son's decision to quit college, especially to play baseball. Furthermore, having seen him essentially sit around and do nothing at the ballpark, Christina was even more dismayed. Now her son was leaving for Hartford, 110 miles (177 kilometers) from New York City. Yet, the son was also supporting his parents, even if by playing a child's game. Gehrig's mother shrugged and began to accept the inevitable.

There was nothing inevitable, however, about Gehrig's future in baseball. First, he had to prove himself. His early weeks at Hartford were not a good omen. Gehrig played poorly on offense and defense.

Luckily, however, Gehrig had found in the Hartford Senators' manager, Paddy O'Connor, a patient, careful coach, who had been instructed by the Yankees to work with Gehrig, to bring him along. "Paddy," Gehrig was to reflect years later, as recounted in *Luckiest Man*, "always took a fatherly interest in me and was always giving me good advice both about baseball and about the way a ballplayer should conduct himself off the field."

Gehrig listened, learned, and improved. So much so that on August 11, the *Hartford Courant* referred to him as "the stealer of Babe Ruth's thunder, the Eastern's Behemoth of Bing, Sultan of Swat, and Kleagle of Klout."

★ ★ ★ ★ ★ ★

YANKEE STADIUM

Before 1923, the year Lou Gehrig signed with the Yankees, there were "parks," "fields," or "grounds," where baseball was played at its leisurely pace, practically in everyone's backyard. Then, there rose a stadium, the first of its kind dedicated to America's pastime. No mere park, this stadium, built by and for the Yankees, was baseball's first triple-decked structure. It could seat 58,000 fans. With Babe Ruth drawing those fans into the game as never before, it was expected that they would crowd such a large venue with little trouble. Soon Yankee Stadium became known as "The House That Ruth Built."

The Yankees would have been content to stay where they were, had they not been kicked out. Beginning in 1913, they had shared the Polo Grounds with its owners, the New York Giants. Then, as the Yankees began to draw bigger and bigger crowds (thanks to the Babe's home runs), the Giants became jealous. When the Yanks outdrew them by more than 100,000 in 1920, the Giants served an eviction notice on their rivals, effective after the 1922 season.

In less than a year, the Yankees built themselves a new stadium, only a mile from the Polo Grounds in the Bronx. Built of 3,000

But then, from August 12 to 21, Gehrig slumped. "I couldn't field, I couldn't hit," he said, as narrated in *Luckiest Man*. He thought he might quit.

No doubt about it, Gehrig was homesick. He missed his mother. After all, she had done everything for him: cooked, cleaned, and told him what a fantastic boy he was. Now, at Hartford, Gehrig was on his own, among some pretty seasoned, even rough, characters. Gehrig needed friends. Given

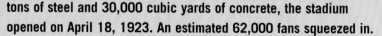

★ ★ ★ ★ ★

tons of steel and 30,000 cubic yards of concrete, the stadium opened on April 18, 1923. An estimated 62,000 fans squeezed in.

The original dimensions at Yankee Stadium were 281 feet (86 meters) down the left-field line; 490 feet (149 meters) to center field; and 295 feet (90 meters) to right field. Center field became know as "Death Valley" because of its great distance from home plate.

In 1932, a monument was erected to Yankees manager Miller Huggins. It was placed in fair territory in deep center field. After the deaths of Ruth and Gehrig, monuments to these two greats were added. In 1976, with an extensive renovation of the stadium completed, a new "Monument Park" was created behind the left-field fence, with many names added. Today, there are 26 honorees, including non-baseball greats who have visited Yankee Stadium, like Pope John Paul II.

The team broke ground in 2006 on a new Yankee Stadium, which is being built across the street from the present stadium. The new ballpark will open in 2009. The design re-creates some of the original stadium's features, and the current field's dimensions will be the same.

Monument Park is behind the left-field fence in Yankee Stadium. Lou Gehrig's monument is at left in the foreground. The park honors 26 people altogether, but only five are commemorated with monuments: Gehrig, Babe Ruth, their manager Miller Huggins, Mickey Mantle, and Joe DiMaggio.

his reserved personality and the fact that he had joined the Senators in mid-season, he was not making any. Furthermore, Gehrig had little money to spend to socialize, choosing instead to send practically every dime he earned to his parents.

Then, on August 22, Gehrig started to hit again. "I decided not to quit after all," he said.

A bit of fatherly advice from O'Connor, as much as improved ballplaying, seemed to have turned young Gehrig's attitude around. "You have a wonderful career ahead of you," the manager told him, according to Jonathan Eig. "But you have to accept the good with the bad. Nothing can stop you, except Lou Gehrig."

MAJOR TRYOUT

A few days before play with the Senators in the Eastern League ended, the Yankees clinched the American League pennant for the third time in a row.

In the 1921 World Series, they had played their crosstown rivals, the Giants, in the first major-league "subway series." The Yankees lost in this last best-of-nine classic.

In 1922, they played the Giants again. The Giants won in five (including one tie).

Now, in 1923, the Yankees would play their archrivals once more.

Huggins, deciding it best to give his players a rest before the World Series opener, brought Gehrig up from the minors to play a few games as the season wound down. Gehrig had done exceedingly well at Hartford, batting .304 and smacking 13 doubles, 8 triples, and 24 home runs. In one stretch, Gehrig hit five homers in seven days.

On September 26, Huggins chose to give first baseman Wally Pipp a rest. Gehrig would start against the Detroit Tigers.

The Yankee pitcher, Bullet Joe Bush, was not pleased with the switch at first base. He wanted to win the game, even if doing so meant little to his team. "Don't put that damn clown out there at first," he yelled for everyone in the dugout to hear, as narrated in *Iron Horse*. "This game may not mean anything to the team, but it means a lot to me. That guy will gum it up."

After a nasty flub, when Gehrig misplayed a bunt, Bullet Joe fumed again. "Ya stupid college punk," he yelled at Gehrig. "Where's your brains, dummy?"

In the eighth inning, with the score 5-2 in favor of Detroit, the Yankees managed to load the bases. It was Gehrig's turn at bat. Bullet screamed, "I wanna win this one. Don't send this kid up there!"

Gehrig proceeded to smash a line drive to the right-field wall for a double, scoring all three runners and tying the game. When a single followed, Gehrig scored the winning run.

Gehrig finished his first major-league season playing 13 games, going to bat 26 times, and hitting .423. He had made the Yankee lineup but only temporarily.

Management was so impressed with the rookie that they tried to add Gehrig to the team's roster for the World Series. The league said no, saying Gehrig had not played enough. Nonetheless, the Yankees went on to win their first World Series, four games to two, over the Giants. With Lou Gehrig now clearly in their future, many more such wins seemed certain.

4

Let the
Streak Begin

On February 29, 1924, rookie Lou Gehrig, along with six other players, boarded a train for New Orleans and the start of spring training. Gehrig carried with him a simple cardboard suitcase and $14 in his pocket.

The previous month, Gehrig had eagerly, perhaps too eagerly, signed his second contract with the Yankees, this one for $2,750. Back then, players could not start drawing their salary until the regular season began. Yes, in spring training their expenses would be covered. Any incidentals, though, any money spent on having a good time, in a city known for providing plenty of opportunity to do just that, would have to be out of pocket. With a six-week stay in the Crescent City looming ahead, $14 was not likely to go far, even for a miser like Gehrig.

To survive on his pittance, Gehrig adopted a simple strategy. He spent practically nothing. "I was glad the team worked out every day from eleven to one," Gehrig was to remark much later, as quoted in *Iron Horse*. "That way I could just skip lunch."

In the evening, Gehrig would often excuse himself from any late-hour fun about town with his teammates. He would leave his hotel room to give them the impression that he had plans. In truth, Gehrig wandered the streets alone with nothing to do.

Gehrig also sought work in the off-hours, any work, to supplement his dwindling stash. No luck. When Miller Huggins, the manager, found out what Gehrig was up to, he summoned the 20-year-old to his office. "Here's $100 as an advance," Huggins said to Gehrig, as recounted in *Luckiest Man*. "Now please stop looking for a job."

Huggins's kindness aside, Gehrig was a rookie, and there were regulars on the team who were not inclined to let him forget his lowly status. Often, Gehrig was rudely crowded out of batting practice—or worse. "Sometimes when I wanted to take some batting practice," Gehrig recalled, as reported in *Luckiest Man*, "I found my favorite bat sawed in four parts, the kind of meanness that was hard to understand."

UNDER OPTION WITH HARTFORD

When spring training ended, the team headed north. Gehrig felt lucky to be on the train. Huggins, typical of what a manager needed to do, had cut his squad. Some rookies were released outright; others were farmed out to other teams. While it was clear that Gehrig was scheduled for another year at Hartford, Huggins, as he had done the year before, wanted Gehrig around Yankee Stadium for a while before sending him packing.

When the time came to slip back to the minors, Gehrig was not at all upset. The *New York Times* described his departure with this observation:

Lou Gehrig, the sensational college slugger from Columbia University, who acquired the title of "second Babe Ruth" by his long hitting with the Yanks last fall and this spring, was sent to the Hartford club in the Eastern League under option yesterday. The youngster was glad to go to a team where he will get needed experience and the Yanks were glad to have him go.

His mother was even resigned to seeing her son off. Ray Robinson, in *Iron Horse*, wrote: "By this time Mom and Pop Gehrig had gotten used to the baseball roller coaster. Since Hartford sounded like Harvard when it went tripping off the tongue, how bad could it be! Also, money was coming in more regularly, and people kept saying such nice things about Lou."

At Hartford, Gehrig sent the ball flying. On June 19, his twenty-first birthday, Gehrig celebrated with a homer, a triple, and a double in a 9-8 victory over Worcester. Gehrig's stats for the rest of the season at Hartford were equally impressive. In 134 games, slugging Lou banged out 37 home runs, 13 triples, 40 doubles, and totaled 134 hits. He batted .369.

While Gehrig was a sensation on offense, his defense was less than big league. Eig, in *Luckiest Man*, summed up Gehrig's problem this way:

First basemen, as a rule, are not the most athletic men on the diamond. They don't have to run as far or fast as outfielders. They don't have to jump and spin as gracefully as shortstops and second basemen. But they've got to be reliable. After the pitcher and catcher, no fielder handles the ball more than the first baseman.

Gehrig understood what needed to be done at first base; it's just that he was still clumsy. Cutoff plays baffled him. Gehrig

Lou Gehrig worked out at first base before a game in 1926 at Yankee Stadium. In his early years, Gehrig was nowhere near as proficient a fielder as he was a hitter. He practiced over and over to improve his defensive skills.

had trouble with the toughest play of all for a first baseman, the backhanded catch. It would take years of practice, which Gehrig was more than willing to put in, before he could perfect his fielding.

PIPP TAKES A FALL

Maybe it was overconfidence. Maybe it was arrogance. Or, maybe it was just an aging workforce. But the 1924 Yankees did not perform as they had the year before. There would be no World Series; there would be no pennant. In fact, in 1924, the Yankees had a miserable season. Miller Huggins would be making changes come the new year.

Nothing much happened in spring training, except that, in 1925, the Yankees moved their operation to St. Petersburg, Florida. Gehrig was there, of course, practicing, playing, and wondering what role, if any, he would ever have as a major-league player.

With the new season under way, Gehrig hung around Yankee Stadium with the team, looking to pinch-hit whenever needed. On June 1, he got his chance.

In the eighth inning, in a game against the Washington Senators, Huggins decided to pull shortstop Pee Wee Wanninger. He put Gehrig in instead. It would be the last time that Gehrig would ever be a pinch hitter. And, it would be the beginning of a 2,130-consecutive-game streak that would give Gehrig his nickname, the "Iron Horse."

On June 2, Gehrig advanced from pinch hitter to regular, when he replaced Wally Pipp at first base. Just how that came about is still open to debate. The most credible story is that Pipp, while taking batting practice, was hit squarely in the head by the batting-practice pitcher, Charlie Caldwell, Jr.

"I just couldn't duck," Pipp recalled in 1953, as detailed in *Iron Horse*. "The ball hit me on the temple. Down I went."

Pipp then supposedly asked Huggins if he could stay out of the game.

In truth, Pipp had been severely injured, so much so that he had to be carted off to the hospital for a two-week recovery.

Pipp's injury gave the Yankee manager the excuse he needed to make a change. The first baseman, who had joined the team in 1915, had been batting only .244, with 3 home runs and 23 runs batted in. Huggins wanted him replaced. Immediately, he turned to Gehrig. "You're my first baseman today," Huggins told him, as reported in *Iron Horse*. "Today—and from now on."

The owner of the New York Yankees, Jacob Ruppert *(second from left)*, met with some of his players in March 1925 during spring training in St. Petersburg, Florida. With him were *(from left)* Babe Ruth, pitcher Bob Shawkey, and Lou Gehrig. Gehrig became the team's starting first baseman during the 1925 season and began his streak of playing in 2,130 consecutive games.

The manager then benched second baseman Aaron Ward, replacing him with Howard Shanks. Next, he canned catcher Wally Schang, putting in Benny Bengough instead. A new lineup was formed, and Gehrig was finally a full-time Yankee. He would remain so every day the team played, for the next 14 years.

BELLYACHING BABE

New players aside, the Yankees were off to a dreadful start as the regular season began. One reason, a critical reason, was the absence of the Babe.

The team had built its success around Babe Ruth's success. He, more than any other player, on any team, set the standard of play. He also set his own standard off the field, one filled with a life of excess in almost every way, particularly when it came to eating.

During spring training, Ruth began to suffer from severe stomach cramps and fever. On April 7, when the team reached Asheville, North Carolina, on its way back from St. Petersburg, Ruth collapsed in a train bathroom. By the time the Yankees' Pullman sleeper reached New York, Ruth was wrapped in blankets and unconscious. His body had to be lifted out of a train window.

"The bellyache heard around the world," newspapers reported in the days to follow, as Ruth settled into what would be a six-week convalescence at St. Vincent's Hospital. According to Frank Graham, in his book *The New York Yankees: An Informal History*, "The immediate cause of the attack was an outlandish early-morning indulgence in hot dogs and soda pop, but behind it were weeks, even months, of free-style eating and drinking. He had absorbed enough punishment off plates and out of bottles to have killed an ordinary man."

On April 17, Ruth had surgery for an intestinal abscess. On May 26, he returned to the Yankees' lineup. Ruth would finish the season with a less-than-stellar batting average of .290, and only 25 home runs in 98 games. It was his worst season in the majors up to that point.

Gehrig, by contrast, was having a superb inaugural year. By season's end, the determined Gehrig had 20 home runs, 68 RBIs, 23 doubles, and 10 triples. He would finish with a respectable .295 batting average. On July 23, Gehrig hit the first of what would come to be 23 professional grand slams. It is a Major League Baseball record that still stands to this day.

★ ★ ★ ★ ★
SPORTS' GREATEST CHALLENGE: SWINGING A BAT

"First of all, the hardest single thing to do in sports is to hit a baseball," said "The Splendid Splinter," Ted Williams. "If this is true and it is, then it takes more hours of practice, more hours of dedication, more hours of desire to hit a baseball than it does to do anything else."

Williams ought to know; he literally wrote the book on the subject, *The Science of Hitting*, published in 1970 and still in print today. With a lifetime batting average of .344, and as the last man to hit above .400 (.406) in a season (1941), Williams made a science of hitting. He believed that batters had a choice; they did not have to swing at anything thrown at them. According to *The 2006 ESPN Baseball Encyclopedia*, "Williams honed his bats to perfection, refined his ideas of the strike zone, thought about whether to swing down or up on the ball, and studied pitchers as if they were helpless butterflies he was about to pin to black paper."

Williams believed that power and plate discipline (discerning strike-zone judgment) were the unbeatable combination that won ball games. He was particularly taken with the force of the walk. He once termed his 2,019 career bases on balls (since corrected to 2,021) as his "proudest record." "Walk, don't run," was a truism Williams was always prepared to put into play.

Burt Shotton, who began his career in 1909 and retired the year Lou Gehrig signed with the Yankees (1923), also loved to walk. "The very name baseball is almost the same as base on balls," he famously said, as noted in *The 2006 ESPN Baseball*

It is hard to know exactly what contributed to the Yankees' demise in 1925, but down they went. The team finished the season in seventh place, with 69 wins and 85 losses. Attendance

☆ ☆ ☆ ☆ ☆ ☆

Encyclopedia. "The spectator at the game is likely to look upon the base on balls as a mere incident; a momentary wildness on the part of the pitcher, or a gift to a dangerous batter. This opinion is often justified, but just as often the base on balls is a real tribute to the batter's skill in working the pitcher."

A player's batting average (BA), slugging percentage (SLG), runs batted in (RBI), on-base percentage (OBP), home runs (HR), and bases on balls (BB) pretty much sum up his hitting prowess. Here, according to *The 2006 ESPN Baseball Encyclopedia*, is how a dozen greats fared in each category:

Name	BA	SLG	RBI	OBP	HR	BB
Hank Aaron	.305	.555	2,297	.374	755	1,402
Ty Cobb	.366	.512	1,938	.433	117	1,249
Joe DiMaggio	.325	.579	1,537	.398	361	790
Lou Gehrig	.340	.632	1,995	.442	493	1,508
Hank Greenberg	.313	.605	1,276	.409	331	852
Reggie Jackson	.262	.490	1,702	.356	563	1,375
Mickey Mantle	.298	.557	1,509	.422	536	1,733
Willie Mays	.302	.557	1,903	.386	660	1,464
Mark McGwire	.263	.588	1,414	.394	583	1,317
Jackie Robinson	.311	.474	734	.409	137	740
Babe Ruth	.342	.690	2,213	.474	714	2,062
Ted Williams	.344	.634	1,839	.482	521	2,021

at Yankee Stadium fell to 697,000, plunging 34 percent from the previous year.

CLUBHOUSE BRAWL

Though Gehrig's success on offense was clearly recognizable, he finally began to show promise on defense as well. For Gehrig, the road to accomplishing his goals was through practice, practice, and more practice. "In the beginning, I used to make one terrible play a game," Gehrig told magazine writer Quentin Reynolds, as quoted in *Iron Horse*. "Then it was one bad play a week, then finally I'd pull a bad one once a month."

It would take some time before Gehrig's fellow players would come to fully appreciate his dogged determination to improve, his relentless desire to succeed by simply working harder. At first, Gehrig was seen by many as a bit too disciplined, too much of a goody-goody. Some were simply put off by his reserved, introverted personality.

It was unlikely his demeanor, and more the realization that Gehrig was a hitter to be reckoned with, that caused opposing pitchers to "play with his head," literally. Gehrig quickly became fair game for the intimidating brushback pitch.

Pitching inside is a favorite weapon, even if there is only the threat of its use. In a game against Detroit, pitcher Earl Whitehill threw a sidearm pitch that almost grazed Gehrig's jaw. Gehrig flew toward the mound, determined to take Whitehill down. The pitcher rushed to home plate. The umpires were quick to intervene but not before Gehrig hurled a challenge, "Come on, if you wanna fight, knock the chip off my shoulder," he relates in *Iron Horse*.

After the game, like kids meeting after school in an alley to have it out, Gehrig and Whitehill let their fists fly. It was quite a clubhouse brawl, with Ty Cobb, Babe Ruth, and a host of other players from both teams joining in. Gehrig was knocked out and had to be carried back to the locker room.

When Gehrig regained full consciousness, he asked those around him, "Who won?" His teammates turned away, telling Gehrig, in effect, that he had misread the situation and over-reacted, and that Whitehill had not intended to hit him with his pitch.

Ray Robinson, in *Iron Horse*, takes a clear-eyed view of where Gehrig stood at this moment in his career: "In 1925 Gehrig was still something of an oversized babe (small 'b') in the woods, one who had a considerable amount to learn about the motivations of opponents who could be expected to play as hard against him as he played against them."

Getting a Grip

In 1926, Lou Gehrig arrived at St. Petersburg to begin his first spring training as a regular Yankee. By all accounts, he was not lugging a cardboard suitcase. But the 22-year-old Gehrig did bring along something most players would have been quick to leave behind—his mother.

For Gehrig, this was payback time. He thought that having his mother travel south in a fancy Pullman railroad car, to bask in the sun for weeks on end, was the least that the tired, worn, 44-year-old Christina deserved. Gehrig was thrilled that he could finally repay his mother for the years of menial work and sacrifice she had known.

Of course, Christina came with an asset that Gehrig, or any ballplayer, would appreciate. Mom could cook. Even though she was "on vacation," Mrs. Gehrig took to preparing big, heavy

German meals, with everything from traditional sauerkraut to pickled eels. In the years to come, Gehrig would bring home his Yankee chums, particularly Babe Ruth, to devour his mother's specially prepared dinners. As Eleanor Gehrig, Lou's future wife, recounts in her book, *My Luke and I*:

> Christina became the "hostess" of the house instead of just the servant. . . . Then, if she needed any more ego-building, it was supplied by Ruth's mighty appetite over her mighty meals—thick vegetable soup, whole suckling pig with apple-in-mouth, potatoes or potato pancakes, double slices of pie and slabs of ultra-heavy cheesecake.

Clearly, Mom was then Gehrig's favorite gal. Actually, she was the only woman in his life. Once, Gehrig made the mistake of confiding in a couple of fellow players that he wanted to meet women but did not know how. They howled at him. "He was just hopeless," Mike Gazella, a backup infielder, recalled, as related in *Luckiest Man*. "When a woman would ask him for an autograph, he would be absolutely paralyzed with embarrassment."

BY HIS ACTIONS

Though still awkward socially, Gehrig was beginning to earn respect through his quiet demeanor and his contrast with the flamboyant Ruth. As the Yankees broke camp and headed north out of Florida, manager Miller Huggins announced, as recounted in *Iron Horse*, "Lou has become an influence to the entire team. You get a player with that kind of spirit and it spreads like a contagion to the other players. He has come around much faster than I dared to expect."

Yet, Gehrig retained a curious trait, one identified far more with childhood than adulthood. When faced with defeat, he would often cry like a baby.

In the eighth inning of a game against the White Sox, Gehrig hit a pop fly for an easy out. Nonetheless, the Yanks rallied and won the game.

The Yankee players boisterously celebrated the team's comeback. Yet, through the shouting, Gehrig's anguished sobbing could be heard. As Robinson tells it in *Iron Horse*, "He [Gehrig] was crying uncontrollably, unable to curb tears of disappointment. Huggins studied Lou for a moment, then in tones not meant to be harsh, said, 'C'mon, Lou, c'mon Lou.'" His teammates had never seen anything like it.

Though a crybaby when he thought he had failed his team, Gehrig could be intimidating in a physical way. In a game with Detroit, the 200-plus-pound Gehrig came barreling into 5-foot-10-inch, 165-pound second baseman Francis "Blackie" O'Rourke.

The umpire judged Gehrig's slide to be interference. O'Rourke picked himself up and shouted some unmentionables at Gehrig. The next day, during infield practice, the two confronted each other. "He was looking as if he was going to bore a hole right through me," Robinson quotes O'Rourke, in *Iron Horse*. Instead of coming to blows, though, Gehrig put out his hand and said, "Frank, I'm sorry I went into you so hard yesterday. I shouldn't have done it." O'Rourke responded in kind. "Forget those names I called you, young fellow," he said. "Lou smiled at me. We were always firm friends after that."

PIANO LEGS

That the Yankees needed a major rebuilding after their disastrous breakdown the previous year, there could be no doubt. Huggins set to work to do just that.

The outfield was in pretty good shape; little change was necessary there. With Bob Meusel in left field, Earle Combs in center, and the Babe in right field, the adept threesome had the grassy expanse of the outfield covered like a glove.

Herb Pennock, the Yanks' veteran pitcher, would be in top form. Two promising youngsters would appear: Myles Thomas, a right-hander, and Garland Braxton, a southpaw. Catchers Pat Collins and Benny Bengough were more than ready to play ball.

It was in the infield that Huggins had serious concerns. Joe Dugan, at third, was the most dependable. Mark Koenig, at shortstop, had but 28 major-league games under his belt when the season commenced and still needed plenty of ripening.

But 28 games were better than none. And none was what rookie second baseman Tony Lazzeri had. Not only that, the youngster, a hot pick from out west in the Pacific Coast League, had never even seen a major-league game. Frank Graham, in his book *The New York Yankees*, illuminates the new ballplayer's look and style:

> He was tall, lean, square-shouldered, and, for all his comparatively slight build, exceedingly strong and durable. He had a face like those in the paintings of the Italian masters—olive-skinned, oval, with high cheekbones and smoldering eyes. He spoke seldom, and when he did his voice had an angry quality, though he was seldom angry.

Graham goes on to say of Lazzeri, "When the race started and the chips were down, he was the one who held the infield together and made the pennant possible."

Gehrig, again, would have an impressive season, with a .313 batting average, 112 RBIs, 135 runs scored, 47 doubles, and 20 triples. Yet, Gehrig's home run total was way off—just 16. It seems that Gehrig, strangely for a left-hander, was hitting almost everything to left field. He should have been pulling the ball to right field. Huggins had to remind Gehrig that he could "pull" any pitcher he wanted. All he had to do was set his mind to doing so.

At the start of the 1926 season, rookie Tony Lazzeri was the biggest question mark on the Yankees. The second baseman, who had played in the Pacific Coast League, had never even seen a major-league game before joining the Yankees. Lazzeri, however, helped to hold the infield together as the Yankees won the American League pennant.

When it came to fielding bunts, Gehrig was a bit off base, too. "Another thing, you don't come in well on bunts," Huggins told him, as recalled in *Iron Horse.* "You never know when to come in or when to stay back and let the pitcher handle the bunt. Work on it every day."

Stealing bases, however, was turning out to be a real Gehrig specialty, all the more surprising for a heavy "Piano Legs" guy like Lou. He would wind up with a career total of 15 steals of home plate, always on the run-scoring end of a double steal.

There would be two such dramatic steals in the 1926 season, both in concert with the Babe. On April 13, in a victory over the Red Sox, the duo pulled it off. Then, on July 24, they did the same in beating the White Sox.

Although stealing bases did not necessarily speed up the game, 1926 saw the fastest game times in the history of the sport. On September 25, in a game that clinched the American League pennant for New York, play was completed in a record 55 minutes. Gehrig homered in the third, while Ruth matched him in the sixth. With today's delaying trips to the mound and ceaseless commercial breaks, it is impossible to imagine two teams finishing up a pro game in less than an hour.

GEHRIG'S FIRST WORLD SERIES

The Yanks had come a long way to win the pennant, hustling and scratching to grab the flag. Given that the Yankees were truly playing as a team, with everyone pulling more than his own weight, yet working together as never before, perhaps it was not such a surprise. Babe Ruth had a fabulous season, rebounding from his illness with little trouble. He led the league in home runs, RBIs, runs scored, bases on balls, and slugging percentage. His batting average was .372, just .006 short of the Triple Crown (a feat he would never accomplish).

The Yankees faced the St. Louis Cardinals in the Fall Classic and took the first game, played at Yankee Stadium on October 2 in front of 61,658 fans. In the sixth inning, the Babe slapped a single to left, moved to second base on a sacrifice, and scored on a Gehrig single, for the 2-1 win. It was the first of Gehrig's record eight game-winning RBIs in World Series play.

Though the Bronx Bombers, as some were now calling the Yanks, had been favored to win the World Series, the Cards

☆ ☆ ☆ ☆ ☆
THE FALL CLASSIC: A HUNDRED YEARS AND COUNTING

In a good omen, the same year that Lou Gehrig was born, baseball decided to formalize what has become known as the Fall Classic, or the World Series. Before 1903, there was postseason play, but it was haphazard, consisting of best-of-five, best-of-seven, and, in 1887, best-of-15 affairs. Often, the series was an intra-league event, between the first- and second-place teams.

Then, in 1903, the champions of the newly formed American League, the Boston Americans (today's Red Sox), and the National League winners, the Pittsburgh Pirates, squared off in a best-of-nine series. Boston won, five games to three. The World Series, as we know it, was born.

The Fall Classic has been played every year but two since its inception. In 1904, the National League winners, the New York Giants, led by their disdainful manager, John McGraw, refused to meet the American League champions, the Boston Americans again, claiming the Giants had nothing to prove. And, 90 years later, in 1994, the Fall Classic went silent during a baseball strike.

It may well have been better had the 1919 World Series not occurred, either. One thing for sure, most fans of the time would just as soon forget the disgrace brought down on the game during that year's postseason play.

succeeded in pushing play to the seventh game. Ruth had hit a three-run homer in Game 4, the first time a player did that in a World Series game. Grover Alexander's clutch pitching had won Games 2 and 6 for the Cardinals.

On October 10, drizzly weather meant that only 38,093 came to Yankee Stadium for the deciding World Series

☆ ☆ ☆ ☆ ☆

The heavily favored Chicago White Sox, meeting the Cincinnati Reds, were upset in eight games in a best-of-nine series. Then, the rumors began to fly. By the end of the following year, eight White Sox players were implicated in the greatest fix in sports history—throwing the World Series. Though never actually convicted of the crime, all eight, including famous, illiterate "Shoeless Joe" Jackson, were barred from the game for life.

Baseball fans were devastated. If it was not for the emergence of Babe Ruth, with his home-run prowess and ability, to pull fans back into the stands, the game may well have stumbled and shuddered for years to come.

Leave it to the Yankees to bring baseball out of its depression, and with them, dominance in the Fall Classic. Since 1921, when the Bronx Bombers won their first pennant, the team has played in 39 of 85 World Series, winning 26. That averages out to nearly a visit every other year and a title every third year. Below is a listing of the years in which the Yankees have played in a World Series, with their wins highlighted:

1921, 1922, 1923, 1926, 1927, 1928, 1932, 1936, 1937, 1938, 1939, 1941, 1942, 1943, 1947, 1949, 1950, 1951, 1952, 1953, 1955, 1956, 1957, 1958, 1960, 1961, 1962, 1963, 1964, 1976, 1977, 1978, 1981, 1996, 1998, 1999, 2000, 2001, 2003

Lou Gehrig is pictured crossing home plate in a 1926 World Series game against the St. Louis Cardinals. The National League champion Cardinals defeated the Yankees in the series, four games to three. Gehrig hit .348 during the seven-game matchup.

contest. More should have come; it was a game to remember, with the game's greatest pitchers facing its greatest sluggers.

With the Cards holding a slim lead, 3-2, in the seventh, their pitcher, Jess Haines, grew tired, and Grover Alexander was pulled from the dugout to finish the game. Some say Alexander had actually been sleeping when he got the summons, but that was unlikely. He jumped right in to do what he could to hold his team's lead.

With the bases loaded for the Yankees, Tony Lazzeri came to the plate. On Alexander's fourth pitch, Lazzeri lined to left field, but the ball went foul, missing a home run by a couple of feet. Lazzeri then struck out, ending the Yankees' rally.

Alexander retired the side in the eighth and the first two men in the ninth. Ruth now came to bat. Alexander walked the Babe. Then, incredibly, Ruth pulled the most famous on-field goof of his career. With Bob Meusel at bat, and Gehrig in the on-deck circle, the Bambino took off trying to steal second base. He was thrown out by catcher Bob O'Farrell. Gehrig clutched his bat and returned to the dugout. The game ended, giving the World Series to the Cardinals.

World champions the Yankees were not. But, in 1926, their squad had been rebuilt. The club had made money. Each player received $3,417.75 as part of his World Series take. And, for some, the off-season would be filled with fun and relaxation.

The Babe went on the vaudeville circuit, earning $8,333 a week for jumping onto the stage through tissue-paper hoops, tossing a baseball around, and attempting a few jokes. By most accounts, it was boring as heck.

Gehrig went home, to his parents' apartment in Morningside Heights. He would spend the winter relaxing, eating Mom's fattening food, and engaging in his favorite sport outside of baseball—fishing. There was always next year. The Yankees would be ready.

6

Murderers' Row

As the 1920s bellowed ahead with gusto, enthusiasm, and opportunity, no year spoke more clearly to what was happening than 1927. To many, 1927 *was* the '20s.

Entertainment, in all its forms, reached out to define the decade. The talking picture *The Jazz Singer* premiered in 1927, to herald the end of silent film and take moving pictures into a whole new realm.

As if to celebrate the emerging sound technology and press the film industry forward, the Academy of Motion Picture Arts and Sciences was founded in 1927. When it handed out its first Oscars, *Wings*, from Paramount Studios, won for best picture.

Of course, the transatlantic solo flight of Charles Lindbergh, on May 20 and 21, 1927, in *The Spirit of St. Louis*, was the year's defining individual accomplishment, even with its entertaining stunt aspect. A hero, it turned out, need not be a movie star or a sports figure to garner public adulation. It did help, though.

While the 1920s was the Roaring Twenties, it was also "The Golden Age of Sports." Players in almost every sport more than exceeded fans' expectations, often becoming heroic legends to millions.

In football, there was Red Grange and Knute Rockne. Tennis had Helen Wills and Bill Tilden. Golf gave the world Bobby Jones and Walter Hagen. Jack Dempsey stood alone as the undisputed heavyweight-boxing champion of the world.

And there would be the Yankees. Soon to avenge their World Series defeat of the previous year, the Yanks would produce in the process a "Murderers' Row," perhaps the finest baseball team that ever played the game. Contributing to their slashing and stomping, Lou Gehrig would have his best year to date.

DOLLARS AND SENSE

Spring training opened with Babe Ruth demanding $80,000 to play ball for the Yankees. Herb Pennock, the team's best pitcher, wanted $20,000, which would, at one-fourth Ruth's ultimatum, make him the second-highest-paid Yankee. The average major leaguer at the time was taking home $10,000 for a year's work tossing and smacking around a five-ounce, leather-coated sphere. The Yankees' front office was ready to offer Gehrig a one-year contract for $8,000—one-tenth the amount "requested" by the Babe.

In turn-of-the-twenty-first-century dollars, Ruth's $80,000 translates to about a million bucks. Compared with what major-league players are getting today, a million dollars does not seem like much. In 1927, though, earning money like that put you in a league all by yourself.

And, for the Sultan of Swat, $80,000 was only part of his take for, well, being the Babe. With Ruth's off-season adventures in moviemaking, vaudeville shows, endorsements, and a ghost-written newspaper column, he was easily earning his salary demands over again.

When the Bambino did settle up and begin what would be his greatest season, he agreed to a reduced compensation. Ruth, it turned out, would be smacking them out of the park for a mere $70,000.

★ ★ ★ ★ ★

BASEBALL TAKES TO THE AIR

Although the first World Series to be broadcast by radio was in 1921, it was with the 1923 Fall Classic, between the Yankees and the Giants, that the medium found its voice—that of announcer Graham McNamee.

As the story goes, McNamee, an aspiring opera singer, was taking a break from jury duty as he passed the studios of radio station WEAF in New York City. On a whim, McNamee went in to see the station manager. He was given an audition and hired on the spot.

At World Series game time, McNamee, who knew little about the sport, was called upon to provide what would eventually be called "color commentary." His descriptions of the action on the field were so engrossing that listeners deluged the station with demands for more. Radio and baseball began a marriage of convenience that continues to this day.

In November 1920, KDKA in Pittsburgh became the first commercial radio station to go on the air. Four others joined it the following year. By 1922, the number of stations leapt to more than 500, and by 1923, to more than 1,000. To tune in to all the chatter, 100,000 radio receivers poured off assembly lines in 1923, and just two years later, an estimated 50 million Americans had access to radio broadcasts.

It is not generally known what Pennock agreed to, but it was probably within a grand or two of $20,000.

With Gehrig, the dollar figure accepted would have been easy to surmise. Whatever he was offered, the Yankees were sure that Gehrig would grab it. And they were right. That did not mean, though, that management could not have a little

☆ ☆ ☆ ☆ ☆ ☆

What were the people to listen to? Certainly not the boring speeches of their presidents, bland characters such as Warren G. Harding and Calvin Coolidge. Folks wanted excitement, action, and vivid descriptions of events. They found all that in sports, particularly baseball. Almost overnight, America's pastime went from the local to the national level. Everyone, it seemed, was tuned in and turned on to baseball.

Here are some sports radio firsts of the 1920s:

- September 6, 1920—first radio broadcast of a prizefight
- November 25, 1920—first radio broadcast of a college football game
- August 5, 1921—first radio broadcast of a baseball game
- August 6, 1921—first radio broadcast of a tennis match
- October 5, 1921—first radio broadcast of a World Series
- November 24, 1923—first radio broadcast of the annual Army-Navy football game
- January 1, 1927—first coast-to-coast radio program, the Rose Bowl Game
- 1929—Harry Hartman becomes the first radio announcer to use the phrase "Going, Going, Gone!" to announce a home run

fun with Gehrig first—and it did. Someone, perhaps it was manager Miller Huggins being directed from on high, began to spread a rumor that the team was searching for a right-handed first baseman. Was this designed to make Gehrig nervous, set him up to be glad for whatever was offered?

Gehrig's response was predictable: "It can't be that anyone who can field any better than I do is needed," he said, as reported in *Iron Horse*. "If there's some mysterious guy who is being considered because he's supposed to be more effective in hitting left-handed pitching, that's a laugh. I can hit lefties as well as right-handers, and just as far."

In the end, Gehrig found himself still on the team—for $8,000. When his contract arrived in the mail, Gehrig read it, signed it, and sent it right back. The money was more than enough to keep his parents from toiling away at grunt work, and that was good enough for him. Gehrig was just happy to have a job in baseball, and with the greatest team in the game at that.

HOME RUN HANDICAP

"Greatest" was indeed the way most fans, sportswriters, and even opposing players were to view the Yankees of 1927. They would win 110 games and lose just 44 to garner the pennant by 19 games. Together, the Yanks batted .307, slugged .489, scored 975 runs, and outscored their opponents by a then-record 376 runs. As it was said, they not only beat their opponents, they demoralized them.

More absorbing for fans than the team's mounting victories was the great American Home Run Handicap being played out by the two ball maulers, "King" Ruth and "Prince" Gehrig. Richards Vidmer, a sportswriter for the *New York Times*, adds flavor to the competition between the two in a piece bemoaning a rain-halted game:

> George Herman Ruth and Henry Louis Gehrig, sometimes
> called the twin thrillers, were specially annoyed by the

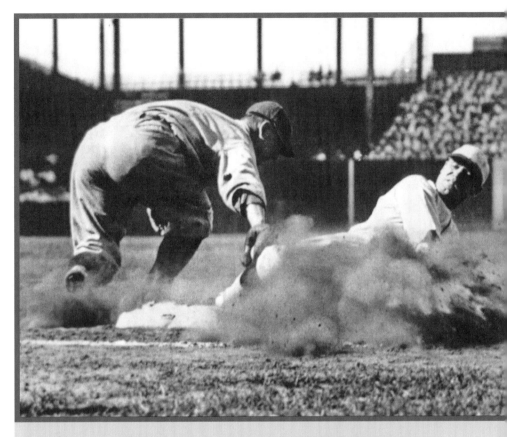

In a 1927 game against the St. Louis Browns, Lou Gehrig put the tag on George Sisler for the out. The 1927 New York Yankees were perhaps the greatest team of all time. They won 110 games and together batted a team average of .307. Gehrig had a year to match the team—winning the American League Most Valuable Player award.

atmospheric conditions. King George fretted and fumed at being restrained in his pursuit of the home run crown which, for the present, is sitting proudly on the head of Prince Louis. The Prince was peeved at the lost opportunity to make the diamond diadem sit more firmly. . . . With the Buster leading the Babe, 35 to 34, sentiment around the circuit seems about evenly divided.

Actually, not so! Fan judgment was not at all split down the middle. In the Home Run Derby, feelings for the Babe clearly ran ahead of admiration for Lou. Vidmer got it right in an earlier *Times* story, with the headline, "Fans Worship Ruth But Forget Gehrig."

This would be the way it would go for Ruth and Gehrig for all their playing days together. The Babe would get all the attention; Gehrig would remain in the shadows.

Yet, the two long-ball slammers, Ruth and Gehrig, now batting third and fourth in the lineup, respectively, remained not only friends throughout the slug fest but also provided each other with visible support that spectators delighted over. Vidmer explains:

> When the Babe hits one for a nonstop flight around the bases, he always finds the Buster waiting with a merry quip and a welcoming hand at the plate. When the Buster hits one and the Babe happens to be on base, they meet at the last stop and chat gaily as they walk to the dugout arm in arm. It's the greatest act in baseball.

But it was not an act. Interestingly, when the two power-hitting Yankees settled down, on long inter-city train rides, to a game of bridge, they always played as partners, never as opponents. They had that much respect for each other.

SERIES SWEEP

While Lou wound up hitting an awesome 47 round-trippers, the Babe easily won the Home Run title by smashing an incredible 60, a single-season record that would stand for 34 years. It was a great way to end the season's competition. But, the crowning achievement for the whole Yankee team was about to commence. The Bronx Bombers would take the World Series in four straight.

Gehrig almost did not make the postseason spectacle, however. Shortly before the series opener, Christina Gehrig became seriously ill. She required surgery to have a goiter (an inflammation of the thyroid) removed, a fairly risky operation. Gehrig threatened to stay by his mother's bedside, even if it meant missing the World Series and breaking what was becoming a noticeable consecutive game-playing streak. "She means more to me," said Gehrig, as reported in *Luckiest Man,* "than any ball game ever invented, even the World Series."

Nonetheless, with assurances from manager Huggins that his mother would be all right and that she did not need Gehrig hanging around the hospital, Gehrig boarded the team train for Pittsburgh on October 3 to meet the Pirates in Game 1 of the World Series. The next day, Christina Gehrig was operated on, and doctors declared the results a success.

The Pirates had a good team, to be sure, but they were doomed from the start. Even with their two tormentors in the outfield, the brothers Paul and Lloyd Waner (otherwise known as "Big Poison" and "Little Poison," respectively), Pittsburgh was simply no match for the Yanks. New York took the first three games with scores of 5-4, 6-2, and 8-1, in that order.

The fourth game did hold some drama. With the score tied, 3-3, in the ninth inning, Gehrig came to the plate with the bases loaded and nobody out. It would be nice to report a storybook finish, with Gehrig hitting one of his 23 career grand slams to win the game and the World Series. It did not happen that way, though. Gehrig struck out. The game ended with a fizzle, not a bang, with Pirates pitcher John Miljus throwing a wild pitch past batter Tony Lazzeri, allowing Earle Combs to come in from third, ending the game. Final score: 4-3.

Though no standout in the World Series, Gehrig contributed mightily to his team's triumphant year, as his individual season stats demonstrate. He batted .373, with 218 hits,

After the Yankees swept the Pittsburgh Pirates in the 1927 World Series, Lou Gehrig and Babe Ruth teamed up to go on a barnstorming tour across the nation. During the season, the two duked it out to see who could hit the most home runs, with the Babe coming out ahead with 60 homers.

52 doubles, 18 triples, and 47 home runs. His 175 RBIs in 1927 set a single-season record at the time. No wonder, following the season, he was voted the American League's Most Valuable Player (MVP).

"BUSTIN' BABE" AND "LARRUPIN' LOU"

"It ain't over 'til it's over" is a saying future Yankee catcher Yogi Berra would make famous. So it was with the 1927 season. Beyond the World Series, there were barnstorming exhibitions for fans in towns and small cities across the country. The 1927 tour would take the Yankees from New York to Ohio to California, with stops in between. Of course, the Babe and the Buster would be going along; it was the "twin thrillers" whom everyone wanted to see.

The team wound up setting barnstorming records, playing before 220,000 fans, traveling 8,000 miles, and autographing 5,000 baseballs. Twenty-one games would be started, but only 13 would be finished. Eight games would never get through the prescribed nine innings. Unbounded enthusiasm and the admiration of uncontrollable spectators ground everything to an untimely halt.

It was that way everywhere the Bustin' Babe and the Larrupin' Lou went. In the exhibition's opening game, in Trenton, New Jersey, the *New York Times* reported: "Twice before the eighth inning, as Ruth lifted the ball over the right field wall, hundreds of boys swarmed into the field to romp from third to home with the King of Swat, each time holding up the game for fifteen minutes before the field could be cleared."

The Babe, being the Babe, loved every minute of these crazy disruptions. "Come all o' yez," Ruth would yell, as he staggered under the weight of an armful of little lads. "Ally opp!"

Gehrig, of course, remained his reserved, controlled self. John Kieran, a *Times* writer, had Gehrig's number when he wrote, on October 26, 1927: "This sturdy and serious lad takes copybook maxims as his guides in life, and lives up to them. 'Strive and succeed.' 'Early to bed, and early to rise.' 'If at first you don't succeed, try, try again.' 'Labor conquers everything.' And all of the rest of them."

Lou Gehrig played the game in his own quiet, out-of-the-spotlight way. "A fine lad," Kieran concluded. "He deserves his success."

In the Shadow of the Babe

With their 1927 combined long-ball total of 107, Babe Ruth and Lou Gehrig out-homered every team in baseball except one. They were the greatest slugging duo the game had ever witnessed.

On the surface, the two had nothing but admiration for the way the other played the game. "One of the finest fellows in the game and a great hitter," the Babe said of Gehrig, as quoted in *Luckiest Man.* "The only real home run hitter that ever lived," returned Gehrig. "I'm just fortunate to be even close to him."

Off the field, their lifestyles could not have been more varied, but still Gehrig's praise never wavered. "It was the most wonderful education I've ever been given," said Gehrig of adventures with Ruth on the road, as recounted in *Iron Horse.* "I don't mean in books. I mean in getting the most out of life, in learning how to meet people and have a good time, and really seeing all there is to see."

Yet the phrase, "The Babe got the headlines; the Iron Horse just got it done," was one that would dog the two all their playing days. Did Gehrig resent the attention Ruth garnered, while he remained second banana? Was he secretly wounded by what some might see as a "spear-carrying" assignment? Probably not, given their opposite personalities. Gehrig could not be like Ruth even if he wanted to be. As Eleanor, Gehrig's future wife, would declare in her autobiography, *My Luke and I*, in referring to Ruth, "You had to look at him and feel that you were watching one of the wonders of the world."

Everyone, it seems, including Gehrig, was willing to accept the reality that Ruth was indeed one of a kind; that there simply would, could, never be anyone else like him.

GET WHAT YOU'RE WORTH

While personalities rarely change or morph into something unrecognizable, a person can grow and mature. As the 1928 season loomed, Gehrig began to display assertiveness not previously in evidence. This was particularly true with regard to salary demands, where it would seem Gehrig was about to utter the "no" word. When his contract arrived in the winter, Gehrig decided not to sign it.

The Babe, who always said no when it came to initial money offers, gave Gehrig stern advice before the Buster even received an offer. "You go in there and ask for what you're worth," he told Gehrig, as related in *Iron Horse*. "I broke the home run record, you knocked in all those darn runs. We've got them where we want them. If I hold out, and you do, too, I'll bet you can get ten thousand more than you expected."

Gehrig promised Ruth that he would turn down anything less than $30,000 a year. That was what he promised. And, he may have actually meant it at the time. Gehrig was

Lou Gehrig and Babe Ruth are seen kidding around during a photo session in 1928. After the 1927 season, Ruth urged Gehrig to toot his own horn, so to speak—telling him to demand what he was worth in his dealings with the Yankees. Before the next season began, Gehrig agreed to a three-year contract worth about $25,000 a year. The long-term deal surprised many.

still Gehrig, however, a man after stability more than money. When push came to shove, in face-to-face "negotiations" with Yankee general manager Edward Barrow and owner Jacob Ruppert, Gehrig pretty much caved in. He emerged with a curious settlement, however. Gehrig would be playing for the Yankees under a three-year contract, for $25,000 a year (about $275,000 in 2006 terms).

The three-year deal surprised many. Why would a promising 24-year-old, who had just hit 47 home runs and won the league's Most Valuable Player award, freeze his salary three years down the line? If Gehrig had been willing to gamble a bit, he might have at least doubled that $25,000 in, say, 1930.

Gehrig, though, was not a bettor. And $25,000 was a king's ransom to him at that point. It would allow Gehrig to buy that nice Colonial-style house in New Rochelle, New York, for his parents. In the end, what did he have to lose? As Ray Robinson put it in *Iron Horse*, "Lou just did not have the stomach to fight the Yankee front office. He'd leave it to Ruth to raise salary standards for himself and others."

Furthermore, as Gehrig would come to appreciate (and the Yankee bean counters regret), a guaranteed $25,000 in 1930, at the beginning of the worst economic disaster in the nation's history, the Great Depression, was a good deal indeed. Gehrig had originally wanted a five-year contract. But three years, it turned out, worked just fine. While many other ballplayers started the depression with reduced compensation, Gehrig found himself in an enviable financial position.

A CHANCE ENCOUNTER

In 1928, the Yankees repeated their triumphs of the year before. They clinched the American League pennant on September 28 and went on to win the World Series, again in four straight, this time against the St. Louis Cardinals.

Both the Babe and the Buster dominated the year's Fall Classic, practically destroying the Cardinals all by themselves.

Gehrig smacked four homers, drove in nine runs, and scored five himself. He batted .545 on six hits.

To better understand Gehrig's increasing power at the plate and the threat it posed to the Cardinals throughout the World Series, it is worth noting that he drew six walks from them, all most likely forced. The Babe walked only once.

Throughout the season, Gehrig's consecutive playing streak continued unabated. He had yet to miss a game. A good thing, too, for had he decided to take a day off from time to time, he might have skipped a particular game against the White Sox, at Chicago's Comiskey Park, late in the year.

Two sisters, Dorothy and Mary Grabiner, needed a ride to the park that day, and they asked one Eleanor Twitchell, a young resident of the Windy City but no lover of the game, to accompany them. They could not drive, but Eleanor could. Of course, Eleanor, though ignorant of baseball's rules and subtleties of play, had heard of Lou Gehrig, the tall, handsome, quiet sensation of the one-and-only Yankees.

"Nice to meet you, ma'am" was Gehrig's shy response, as quoted in *Iron Horse*, when he was quickly introduced to Eleanor, as he exited the playing field after batting practice. He then immediately made a beeline for the dugout.

Eleanor, for the rest of her life, had difficulty recalling exactly what occurred that day. Lou, however, insisted that things happened as described.

It would seem, as observed by Ray Robinson, that "the mighty sequoia of the Yankees, the first ballplayer Eleanor had ever met, made as much an impression on her that afternoon as some faceless stranger sitting next to her on the Chicago elevated." In five years the two would marry.

BREAK UP THE YANKEES

No sooner had the 1928 World Series concluded than the cry went out from sportswriters everywhere, "Break up the Yankees." So dominant and all-powerful had the team become,

Yankees manager Miller Huggins contemplated the action during a game in August 1928 in Yankee Stadium. His death late the following season devastated the Yankees and Lou Gehrig. "There was never a more patient or pleasant man to work for," Gehrig said about Huggins.

that many, in and out of baseball, saw no room for other teams to truly compete. It was feared that as long as the Yankees continued to play as they had been, they would go on winning indefinitely; no one else would have a chance. At least one of the team's major sluggers ought to be traded, it was reasoned. "Having Ruth and Gehrig on the same team was superfluous,"

Jonathan Eig clarified. "Like having Charles Lindbergh and Amelia Earhart in the cockpit of the same plane."

Gehrig, it seemed, was the logical choice to go. This time, Gehrig did not panic. He knew he was not heading anywhere. Huggins soon soothed his players and the public. He gave the front-office position by stating, as related in *The New York Yankees*, "It won't be necessary to break up the Yankees. No matter what we do, the law of averages will take care of us. We can go on, trying to improve the team to the best of our ability. But the time will come when we will crash."

And, indeed, in 1929, crash they did, along with, sadly, their manager. Huggins was a constant worrier, and his health had been slipping all season. On September 20, he arrived at Yankee Stadium so weak he could hardly get into his uniform. On September 25, the fiery manager, who loved baseball and the Yankees more than anything, died of erysipelas, an infectious disease. The team was devastated, no one as much as Gehrig.

"I guess I'll miss him more than anyone else," he said, as recounted in *Iron Horse*. "Next to my mother and father, he was the best friend a boy could have. . . . There was never a more patient or pleasant man to work for. I can't believe he'll never join us again."

HOME RUN BUMMER

Of course, the Yankees were not the only ones to crash in 1929, after finishing 18 games behind the Philadelphia Athletics. On Tuesday, October 29, the stock market crumbled, losing about $26 billion in market share. The nation would begin its long, agonizing economic nightmare, during which, at one point, 25 percent of the workforce would be out of a job.

Fortunately, thanks to Huggins's excellent financial advice, most Yankee players were not heavily invested in the stock market. No Yankee need be jumping out of a window in economic despair.

Though the Yankees would be denied pennant wins in the years '29, '30, and '31, Gehrig played on, never missing a game and turning in some impressive stats. In 1930, he led the

☆ ☆ ☆ ☆ ☆

DOWN BUT NOT OUT: BASEBALL DURING THE GREAT DEPRESSION

In 1932, as the Great Depression gained full force, Babe Ruth, ever the forceful negotiator, demanded his typical $80,000 salary. When asked by the press how it was that he could justify getting paid more than Herbert Hoover, the president of the United States, the Babe replied, "I had a better year than Hoover did, didn't I?"

Actually, Ruth had had a better year than most Americans could dream of. In the same year, the average working American earned $1,300. U.S. manufacturing output had fallen to 54 percent of its 1929 level. Unemployment was affecting 12 million to 15 million workers, or 25 to 30 percent of the workforce. The nation's economic calamity would last through the decade.

Naturally, when a fan had to decide between a meal and a stadium ticket, attendance at ballparks fell. By 1933, it was down 40 to 45 percent. Players' salaries, even the Babe's, took a plunge. Teams eliminated players, and minor-league teams folded altogether to half their pre-depression number. Team owners suffered a collective loss margin of close to 24 percent.

With players in a severely weakened bargaining position, they were forced to withstand tough conditions just to stay in the game, on the roster, and employed. Doubleheaders in the heat of summer were a common occurrence. Grueling train rides to any city that could draw a crowd were the order of the day. If you did not like it, if you were not prepared to play through all manner of

league in RBIs, with 174. The following year he did the same, with an additional 10 runs batted in, a total of 184. In 1931, Gehrig hit 46 home runs, the same number as Ruth. Gehrig's

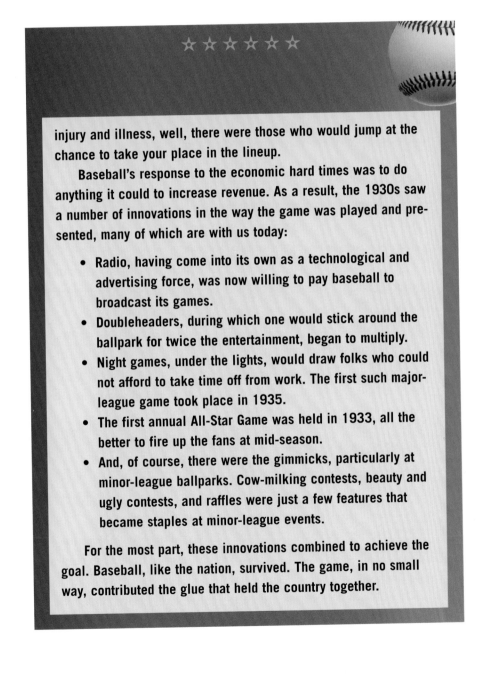

★ ★ ★ ★ ★

injury and illness, well, there were those who would jump at the chance to take your place in the lineup.

Baseball's response to the economic hard times was to do anything it could to increase revenue. As a result, the 1930s saw a number of innovations in the way the game was played and presented, many of which are with us today:

- Radio, having come into its own as a technological and advertising force, was now willing to pay baseball to broadcast its games.
- Doubleheaders, during which one would stick around the ballpark for twice the entertainment, began to multiply.
- Night games, under the lights, would draw folks who could not afford to take time off from work. The first such major-league game took place in 1935.
- The first annual All-Star Game was held in 1933, all the better to fire up the fans at mid-season.
- And, of course, there were the gimmicks, particularly at minor-league ballparks. Cow-milking contests, beauty and ugly contests, and raffles were just a few features that became staples at minor-league events.

For the most part, these innovations combined to achieve the goal. Baseball, like the nation, survived. The game, in no small way, contributed the glue that held the country together.

consecutive-game streak? Not that many people, including Gehrig, had noticed yet, but with the conclusion of the 1931 season, it stood at 1,042.

The 1932 season would turn out to be a great one for the Yankees, and a dramatic one for Gehrig, not to mention Ruth.

On June 3, 1932, in a game against the rival Athletics, Gehrig had what might be considered his best single day on the baseball diamond. In the first inning, he smacked a two-run homer to left-center field. In the fourth inning, he hit another home run. And in the next inning, Gehrig smashed his third fence-jumper of the day, again to left-center field.

For the fourth time in his career, Gehrig had hit three home runs in one game. He wasn't through yet. In the seventh inning, Gehrig clobbered a fastball over the left-field fence for number four. That tied a record for the number of home runs in a single game. No one had ever hit five.

Though Gehrig would come to the plate two more times in the game and hit one deep, deep, deep into center field, five was not to be. That fiery pellet was intercepted by Al Simmons, who had been switched from left to center field earlier in the game.

"You know," Gehrig said after the game, as recounted in *Luckiest Man*, "I think that last one was the hardest ball I hit all day. Gosh, it felt good. . . . I wonder what Mom and Pop up at New Rochelle thought of it. Too bad Mom didn't see it."

THE "CALLED SHOT"

With their new manager, Joe McCarthy, the Yankees were back on top in 1932, winning 107 games while losing just 47. They would meet the Chicago Cubs in the World Series.

The series itself was a typical Yankee slaughter. They dispatched the Cubs in four games, averaging more than nine runs a game.

It would have been a "ho-hum" Fall Classic, however, even for New York fans, if it had not been for Game 3 and an event still talked about and debated to this day.

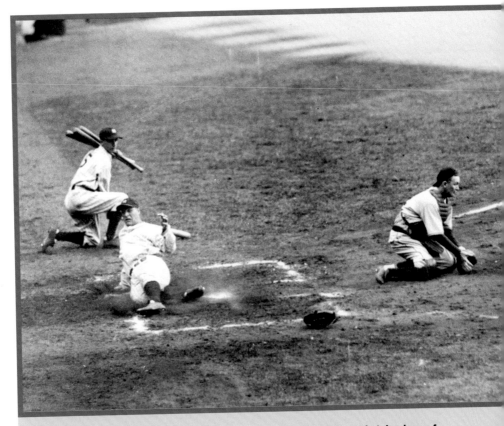

Sliding into home plate, Lou Gehrig scored during the third inning of Game 2 of the 1932 World Series. The Yankees swept the Chicago Cubs for their first world championship since 1928. The series was perhaps best known for Babe Ruth's "called shot" home run in Game 3. Gehrig also slugged a homer right after him, but the Babe's hit garnered the spotlight.

Ruth's called shot, which may or may not have actually been meant as such, is best summed up by Frank Graham, in his book *The New York Yankees*:

It was in this game that the Babe contributed his astonishing achievement of calling his shot on Charlie Root, the Cubs' starting pitcher. In the fifth inning, Root ripped a fastball across the plate; and the Babe, without waiting for the umpire, called a strike on himself, holding up one finger in derision as he grinned at the Cubs' bench. Another fastball split the plate, and the Babe called that, also, holding up two fingers. Now the crowd was howling, and the Cubs in the dugout were jeering. And now the Babe, with a wave of his right arm, indicated that he would hit the next pitch over the wall in right center.

And, that is exactly what the incomparable Babe Ruth did.

What few remember, however, is that immediately after Ruth's home run, Gehrig stepped to the plate to act on advice that the Babe had whispered to him as he tagged home from his called shot. Ruth told Gehrig to do the same thing. Although Gehrig would never think of calling a shot, he did as ordered and smacked his second home run of the game.

Though Gehrig's homer clearly won the game, few recall the event. "Let's face it," Gehrig said, as reported on *Lou Gehrig: The Official Web Site*, "I'm not a headline guy. I always knew that as long as I was following Babe to the plate I could have gone up there and stood on my head. No one would have noticed the difference. When the Babe was through swinging, whether he hit one or fanned, nobody paid any attention to the next hitter. They all were talking about what the Babe had done."

As always, the Babe got the headlines; the Iron Horse just got the job done.

New Gal
in Town

Worn out from a hard day at the office in 1931, Eleanor Twitchell boarded an afternoon trolley and headed home to her South Side Chicago apartment. Though she was glad for her $40-a-week job during the deepening Great Depression, working as a secretary at the Chicago World's Fair headquarters was tiresome for the 25-year-old "toddlin' town" resident. As Eleanor climbed the outer steps to her apartment building, she spotted an old friend and poker-playing neighbor, Kitty McHie, as the woman backed into her flat, arms laden with beer bottles. "Drop over later for some beer because Lou Gehrig's coming over," McHie shouted off-handedly, as Eleanor relates in her autobiography, *My Luke and I.*

It is doubtful that in accepting her neighbor's invitation to the party, Eleanor conjured up an image of her first meeting with Gehrig, fleeting as it was, back in 1928. More likely, the beer and the knowledge that Gehrig was now, as she put it in *My Luke and I*, "big, handsome, and successful," were the draw. Yes, to the party the never-that-tired Eleanor would go.

The previously unrestrained Miss Twitchell was now ready to settle down, to find that special someone. She had had it pretty good before the economic downturn, a truly Roaring Twenties gal. "I was young and rather innocent," she recalls in *My Luke and I*. "But I smoked, played poker, drank bathtub gin along with everybody else, collected $5 a week in allowance from my father, and spent $100." Clearly, Eleanor Twitchell was no Lou Gehrig. If opposites attract, though, then something was bound to happen at McHie's party that evening. Something did.

"The 'shy one' suddenly became the bold one, singled me out and spent the whole time giving me a shy man's version of the rush," Eleanor remembers in her autobiography. Gehrig, in town for a game against the White Sox, was clearly smitten.

Come midnight, however, the flirtations had to cease. Yankee curfew was in effect, and Gehrig was not about to violate it. "I think we were falling slightly in love that night," Eleanor recalls, "but I was no match for his curfew." Gehrig did ask if he could escort Eleanor home. A few blocks from her door, however, Gehrig abruptly said goodnight and disappeared into the dark, not even attempting a departing kiss.

MOVE OVER, MOTHER

Soon they began to exchange letters. "The notes were fairly noncommittal for a couple of people who already were taken with each other," Eleanor wrote in *My Luke and I*. "He didn't bother to tell me that he was going to Rye Beach amusement park every night when the Yankees were home, buying a fistful of tickets for the roller coaster to get his 'highs' and 'lows' by himself. And I didn't tell him my boyfriends were suddenly looking small by comparison."

Lou Gehrig and Eleanor Twitchell, then his fiancée, talked before a game in June 1933 at Comiskey Park in Chicago. They were married three months later. Twitchell was from Chicago, where the two met.

Eleanor doesn't remember who proposed to whom. "We just plotted and planned," she recalls.

The scheming included what to do about Mom. "That" problem, as Eleanor called it. "I hadn't had very much experience with mothers-in-law," she recounts in her autobiography.

"So at Lou's suggestion I invited Mrs. Gehrig to be my guest in Chicago."

Mother came, but the few days the two spent together did not go well. "This was becoming a good old-fashioned triangle—me, my man, and my man's mother," Eleanor summarized in *My Luke and I.* "There was his mother, strenuously fighting to preserve all the ties that bind. Classic case, classic dilemma."

The wedding itself, on September 29, 1933, was a modest civil affair; all the better to get over quickly an event that Gehrig's mother might not, and as it turned out, did not attend.

Moving the wedding date up, however, meant the original plan of marrying after the American League season ended had to be scrapped. After the ceremony, the couple changed clothes, and then with a motorcycle escort, made it to Yankee Stadium in time for Gehrig to take the field. The streak remained uninterrupted—at 1,350.

CULTURAL AWAKENING

After their wedding, the couple settled into their own apartment, a block from Lou's parents, in New Rochelle, New York. As close to mother and father as the Gehrigs were, at least they had not moved in, as Christina would have preferred. In fact, from this moment on, Luke, as Eleanor liked to call her husband, made it clear who was the new number-one gal in his life. "'Eleanor will come first,'" his wife reported Luke saying. "It was that direct and that decisive."

In the months to come, Eleanor tried, with considerable success, to expand her Luke's world, to provide a cultural awakening. Opera was the starting point.

Luke was game. He had only one stipulation. As Eleanor tells it in *My Luke and I,* "Ballplayers are targets for all kinds of heckling from the guys in the other dugout during the summer and, if it got around the American League that Gehrig had become an opera buff during the winter, he could be totally certain of one thing—every time he went to bat, he'd hear a chorus of the most shrieking off-key arias and yodeling imaginable. Anything to rattle the man going to the plate."

So, the Gehrigs made a pact—they would creep into and out of the opera house as inconspicuously as possible.

Gehrig's acceptance, even love, of opera may have stemmed from the simple fact that he could understand what the performers were singing about. Many operas at the time were in German, and Gehrig spoke the language fluently.

After the 1934 season, a number of Yankees headed out for a barnstorming tour like no other, with games to be played in Japan and in Manila in the Philippines. Yankees owner Jacob Ruppert had not wanted Gehrig to go, fearing injury. But Gehrig had promised Eleanor a belated honeymoon, albeit a working honeymoon, and here it was. Before the couple returned to New York on February 14, 1935, they had traveled around the world, stopping in places such as Singapore, Ceylon, Bombay, Cairo, Naples, Rome, Paris, and London. Gehrig's cultural awakening had blossomed into full bloom.

OUT OF THE SHADOW

While the Japan tour was a great hit for all the Yankees who made the trip, it was particularly sweet for Babe Ruth—bittersweet. He was the star, as usual, everywhere he went. The same could not be said for his 1934 season with the Yankees, however. Ruth continued a downward slide begun early in April. By year's end, the Babe had hit but 22 homers, knocked in only 84 runs, and batted only .288. The season would be Ruth's last as a Yankee.

Gehrig, by contrast, was having a terrific time as a Bronx Bomber, though a mid-season minor-league exhibition game, played in Norfolk, Virginia, almost ended his career.

Ray White was pitching for the Norfolk Tars when he threw a fastball high and inside, and straight at Gehrig's head. The ball smacked Gehrig about two inches above the right eye and

Here, Lou Gehrig takes a seat on the bench—the piano bench. His marriage to Eleanor opened up new worlds to him. They began to go to the opera, and after a barnstorming tour in the Far East, the couple took a belated honeymoon to places like Bombay, Cairo, and Paris.

then bounced into the air, almost to the grandstand. Gehrig collapsed like a string puppet with its threads suddenly cut.

White thought he had ended Gehrig's streak and even bragged about the possibility. White, though, did not know Gehrig. The next day the Buster was back in the lineup, wearing one of the Babe's large caps, all the better to conceal a huge bump on his head.

On November 3, 1934, Lou Gehrig won the Triple Crown, the first Yankee to capture the honor. He led the league in homers (49), runs batted in (165), and batting average (.363).

If that was not accomplishment enough for the slugging, plodding, dependable Gehrig, on April 12, at the start of the 1935 season, he was made team captain. The last Yankees captain had been Babe Ruth. With the Babe now gone—he was playing for the Boston Braves—and Gehrig having won the Triple Crown, the Iron Horse, the team's tower of locomotive strength and durability, was ready to step out of the shadows and into the spotlight—or so it would seem.

MEDIA MADNESS

With all his success as a Yankee in 1934, it was expected that Gehrig would ask for a sizable salary to begin the 1935 season. Indeed, no sooner had Lou and Eleanor's cruise ship, the *Berengaria*, docked and its passengers disembarked upon its return from the Far East than reporters immediately peppered Gehrig with questions about what he expected to be paid for his services as a Yankee.

"You know," Gehrig told Roscoe McGowen of the *New York Times*, "I've got a new manager now," referring to his wife. "We feel that I've earned something on the record that's behind me and the one that's yet to be made. I had a big year in 1934. . . . I won't be 32 until June and I figure I've still got my best years ahead of me."

Gehrig asked for $35,000. Ruppert, the Yankee owner, countered with $27,000. They settled quickly on $31,000—a

☆ ☆ ☆ ☆ ☆ ☆

TRIPLE CROWN: ALL TRY, FEW EVEN COME CLOSE

When a player wins baseball's batting Triple Crown, he receives nothing—nothing tangible, that is. There is no plaque, no trophy. The award, though, is the highest honor a batter can achieve. To become a Triple Crown winner in the American or National League, he must, at season's end, lead in three categories: home runs, batting average, and runs batted in. Only a dozen players have done it since 1894, although two, Rogers Hornsby and Ted Williams, have accomplished the feat twice.

Here is a listing of the winners, according to the *2006 ESPN Baseball Encyclopedia*, with the year won, league, team, and stats:

Name	Year	League	Team	HR	BA	RBI
Hugh Duffy	1894	National	Boston	18	.438	145
Nap Lajoie	1901	American	Philadelphia	14	.426	125
Ty Cobb	1909	American	Detroit	9	.377	107
Rogers Hornsby	1922	National	St. Louis	42	.401	152
Rogers Hornsby	1925	National	St. Louis	39	.403	143
Chuck Klein	1933	National	Philadelphia	28	.368	120
Jimmie Foxx	1933	American	Philadelphia	48	.356	163
Lou Gehrig	1934	American	New York	49	.363	165
Joe Medwick	1937	National	St. Louis	31	.374	154
Ted Williams	1942	American	Boston	36	.356	137
Ted Williams	1947	American	Boston	32	.343	114
Mickey Mantle	1956	American	New York	52	.353	130
Frank Robinson	1966	American	Baltimore	49	.316	122
Carl Yastrzemski	1967	American	Boston	44	.326	121

Lou Gehrig received a trophy on August 17, 1933, in St. Louis when he played his 1,308th consecutive game—breaking the record previously held by Everett Scott. With him at the ceremony were *(from left)* William Harridge, president of the American League; Edgar G. Brands, a St. Louis journalist; and teammate Joe Sewell. The following year, Gehrig won the Triple Crown, leading the league in batting average, home runs, and runs batted in.

princely sum in the midst of the Great Depression, and one that made Gehrig the highest-paid player in baseball.

Besides, as the Babe had demonstrated (and Gehrig was about to discover), additional money could be made trading on your star status as a major-league baseball player.

An amusing incident illustrates Gehrig's product endorsement adventures, limited as they turned out to be. Gehrig had signed a contract with Quaker Oats to promote its Huskies cereal. Appearing on Robert L. Ripley's *Believe It or Not*, a coast-to-coast radio show, the host asked Gehrig what made him so strong, so able to hit all those homers? What did the Iron Man eat for breakfast? Gehrig, though a bit nervous, responded on cue, as related in *Iron Horse*, "A heaping bowlful of Wheaties!"

Wheaties! Wrong cereal, wrong company! Wheaties was a product of General Mills.

Gehrig felt humiliated. He offered to return the $1,000. Quaker Oats, recognizing a publicity windfall, would have none of it. The company invited Gehrig back on the show and asked him the same question again. "My favorite is Huskies," Gehrig eagerly announced, "and I have tried them all."

The Yankees did not win the pennant in 1935, but Gehrig had a solid year, with a respectable home-run total of 30, 119 runs batted in, and a batting average of .329. The only down side was Gehrig's recurring attacks of what was thought to be lumbago, an affliction of the lower back. In an August 5 game against the Red Sox, the pain was so great, Gehrig had to bench himself in the fourth inning.

Iron Horse

With the departure of the Sultan of Swat, at the conclusion of the 1934 baseball season, the sun, it would seem, was at last ready to shine its full brilliance on Lou Gehrig. And, indeed, for a brief time, through 1935, it did. Yet no sooner had Gehrig begun to feel the warm rays of attention than a new moon appeared to eclipse his accomplishments once more.

In the early spring of 1936, three men left San Francisco for a cross-country car trip that would, a week later, deposit them at the Yankees training camp in St. Petersburg, Florida. Frank Crosetti and Tony Lazzeri were Yankee veterans. The third man, but 21 years old, and in effect hitching a ride because he could not drive, was the team's latest rookie.

Joe DiMaggio was no ordinary recruit. In his first year with the San Francisco Seals of the Pacific Coast League,

DiMaggio—"a gawky, awkward kid, all arms and legs like a colt, and inclined to be surly" (as one writer described him as an 18-year-old)—batted safely in 61 consecutive games. He was the talk of the minor leagues. Now, having signed with the Yankees, the youngster was headed east, the newest new Babe.

Indeed, DiMaggio enjoyed a fabulous first year as a Yankee. He hit 29 home runs, had 125 RBIs, and batted .323. He was worth every penny of his $8,500 salary, and the fans knew it. A typical *New York Times* headline of the season cried out, "Yanks Score, 12-3, as DiMaggio Stars."

Yet Gehrig, who received little press notice, had an even more impressive year, as the Yanks went on to take the pennant and the World Series. In 1936, Gehrig hit 49 homers, chalked up 152 RBIs, and averaged .354. He won his second American League Most Valuable Player award.

"It seemed a terrible shame for Lou," his teammate, pitcher Lefty Gomez, said of that comeback season for the Bronx Bombers. "Joe became the team's biggest star almost from the moment he hit the Yanks."

Nonetheless, on a personal level, Gehrig displayed no ill feelings toward DiMaggio. From the start, Gehrig was his genuine, candid self. "Lou Gehrig came over to me, slapped me on the back and said, 'Nice to have you with us, Joe,'" DiMaggio recalls of their first meeting in spring training, in his autobiography, *Lucky to Be a Yankee*. "He spoke in that natural, sincere way of his and there was no doubt that he meant it."

GREATEST MOMENT

For the next four years, beginning in 1936, the Yankees dominated Major League Baseball as never before. They would win four consecutive World Series—a record at the time. Although DiMaggio was a real asset to the team during these years, so, too, was Gehrig. At least he was for the first two seasons.

The World Series of 1936 was particularly sweet for Gehrig. Before the games began, with their crosstown rivals the Giants,

Lou Gehrig got a rare smile out of rookie Joe DiMaggio during spring training in 1936 in St. Petersburg, Florida. DiMaggio had a sensational rookie season. Gehrig had an even more spectacular year, although DiMaggio seemed to capture the headlines.

Gehrig shared the cover of *Time* magazine with Giants pitcher Carl Hubbell. Hubbell was considered to have the best screwball in the game. During the season, he won an astonishing 26 games, while losing only 6. Hubbell's earned-run average was an incredible 2.31. Slugger Lou Gehrig and pitching ace Carl Hubbell—the World Series promised to be quite a duel.

At the end of three games, the Yanks led 2-1. Hubbell had pitched the first game, winning it, 6-1. Now on the mound again, in the fourth matchup, he felt this was it. Hubbell had to win if the Giants had any chance for a championship.

In the third inning, Gehrig stepped into the batter's box. Soon the count went to three-and-one. Gehrig did not have to swing at the next pitch. With a three-and-one count, a batter can take or leave what comes his way next. Hubbell heaved a curveball high and inside, so inside it nearly grazed Gehrig's ear. As far as the pitcher was concerned, it was practically an intentional walk.

To the surprise of everyone in both camps, Gehrig took a swing. Moments later the ball was bouncing into the right-field bleachers. The Yanks went on to win, 5-2.

"I have had thrills galore," Gehrig later said, as quoted in *Iron Horse*. "But I don't think any of them top that one." Little did he know, such "highs" would soon become a thing of the past.

GEHRIG GOES HOLLYWOOD

Maybe Gehrig really did want the attention, a chance to shine. If the media would not give him his due playing baseball, perhaps Hollywood was his ticket to notoriety. Other sports figures had made a splash, if only fleetingly, in the movies. The Babe had done it. Why not Gehrig? He was tall, handsome, an all-American boy with instant name recognition. Of course, he knew nothing about acting. And, while Gehrig had a pleasant enough voice, he was hardly Orson Welles. "Yes," thought Lou (or at least his agent, Christy Walsh, did), why not Gehrig on the big screen?

What role would Gehrig play? Tarzan came instantly to mind. Hollywood expressed interest, but first, movie execs wanted to see how Gehrig looked in a leopard-skin loin-cloth, out of his baggy, flannel pants. When they did, they were shocked. Jonathan Eig explains the overall reaction, in *Luckiest Man*, "Yet while his upper body looked like some-thing out of an anatomy textbook, his lower body appeared

Monte Pearson, the winning pitcher of Game 4 in the 1936 World Series, and Lou Gehrig posed for photographs in the locker room after the game. Gehrig hit a home run off New York Giants ace Carl Hubbell to help the Yankees win the game. The Yanks would go on to capture the World Series, too.

to belong to another species, neither man nor ape. Each thigh was bigger than many a man's waist, each calf the size of a Christmas ham."

☆ ☆ ☆ ☆ ☆ ☆

THE ALL-STAR GAME: A NOVEL IDEA IS A BIG HIT

On the sweltering afternoon of July 6, 1933, at Comiskey Park in Chicago, 47,595 baseball fans gathered to witness the antics of the game's most glittering assemblage of ball-playing talent ever gathered. The first All-Star Game pitted the best of the National League, led by manager John McGraw, against the finest the American League could muster, headed by manager Connie Mack. The idea was novel, billed as a one-time deal to help boost attendance at the Chicago World's Fair. So successful was the initial event, won by the American League, 4-2, that the game has been played as a "Midsummer Classic" ever since.

Through 2006, the National League has won 40 games, and the American League has taken 35 games, with two ties. The American League has been dominant for much of the last two decades, while the National League was the stronger team in the 1960s and '70s.

Selected by managers and fans, the first game in 1933 included an impressive list of greats. From the National League came Dick Bartell, Chick Hafey, and Chuck Klein. From the American League, Lou Gehrig was at first and Lefty Gomez was the starting pitcher. And, of course, there was the Babe. As Wild Bill Hallahan, the National League's starting pitcher, put it, according to the *All-Star Baseball Almanac*, "We wanted to see the Babe. Sure, he was old and had a big waistline, but that didn't make any difference. We were on the same field as Babe Ruth."

Here are the 1933 National and American League All-Star starting lineups:

Tarzan, Gehrig was not to be.

Walsh kept trying. He eventually had Gehrig signed to a one-movie deal. Filming would begin after the 1937 baseball

☆ ☆ ☆ ☆ ☆

NATIONAL LEAGUE

Batting Order	Name	Team	Position
1	Pepper Martin	St. Louis Cardinals	3B
2	Frankie Frisch	St. Louis Cardinals	2B
3	Chuck Klein	Philadelphia Phillies	OF
4	Chick Hafey	Cincinnati Reds	OF
5	Bill Terry	New York Giants	1B
6	Wally Berger	Boston Braves	OF
7	Dick Bartell	Philadelphia Phillies	SS
8	Jimmie Wilson	St. Louis Cardinals	C
9	Bill Hallahan	St. Louis Cardinals	P

AMERICAN LEAGUE

Batting Order	Name	Team	Position
1	Ben Chapman	New York Yankees	OF
2	Charlie Gehringer	Detroit Tigers	2B
3	Babe Ruth	New York Yankees	OF
4	Lou Gehrig	New York Yankees	1B
5	Al Simmons	Chicago White Sox	OF
6	Jimmy Dykes	Chicago White Sox	3B
7	Joe Cronin	Washington Senators	SS
8	Rick Ferrell	Boston Red Sox	C
9	Lefty Gomez	New York Yankees	P

season, with Gehrig playing a sort of urban cowboy, rounding up bad guys in a movie called *Rawhide.* The script, with the star wearing long pants throughout, suited Gehrig just fine. The girl in the film was supposed to be his sister, thus Gehrig would never have to pucker his lips for a kiss. Eleanor, back home in New York, need have nothing to fret about.

SOMETHING'S NOT RIGHT

Hollywood "success" aside, as 1937 faded, so did Lou Gehrig. All players have slumps, and Gehrig had certainly seen his share over a dozen years as a Yankee. But, when his latest slump appeared, in the waning weeks of the season, somehow this one felt different. "I don't seem to be timing the ball right," Gehrig said. One teammate thought he looked as if his strength had been sapped.

At the start of spring training, in mid-March 1938, Gehrig felt plain lousy. More ominously, his hands began to ache, with blisters and bruises appearing. That could mean Gehrig was grabbing the bat too tightly, perhaps compensating for muscle loss in his legs, hips, and shoulders.

As league play got under way, Gehrig continued to have problems. In one eight-game stretch, he hit but four times. As he logged his 1,971st consecutive game, it was clear that Lou Gehrig had become a weaker, less talented man than a few months before.

On May 31, 1938, the day Lou was to play in his 2,000th uninterrupted game, his wife, Eleanor, hit her husband between the eyes with a bold, out-of-the-blue suggestion. "Lou," she recounted in *My Luke and I,* "I've got an idea. Don't go to the Stadium today. Tell them anything you want, but skip it."

Gehrig stood dumbfounded at what he was hearing. "Look," Eleanor continued, "if you are worried about the streak, think how they'll remember a streak that stopped at 1,999 games in a row. That's a lot more memorable than 2,000."

Gehrig, of course, would have none of it. He silently shook his head, walked out the door, and made a beeline for Yankee Stadium.

WHEN ENOUGH IS ENOUGH

On April 30, 1939, the New York World's Fair opened with the hopeful purpose of lifting the city and country out of the Great Depression. Exhibits featured television broadcasts, a keyboard-operated speech synthesizer, and a streamlined pencil sharpener. The fair's theme, "The World of Tomorrow," was all about progress, hope, and a brighter future. It was about making life better.

For Lou Gehrig, however, tomorrow was beginning to look anything but bright. He continued to falter—badly.

One day, pitcher Wes Farrell was in the clubhouse when he noticed Gehrig trying, with extreme difficulty, to get up on a bench to look out a window. "All of a sudden," recalled Ferrell, as reported in *Iron Horse*, "he fell backward, down to the floor. He fell hard, too, and lay there frowning, like he couldn't understand what was going on."

Then, the next day Gehrig went to the St. Petersburg golf course. Instead of wearing cleats, he had on ordinary sneakers, all the better to slide his feet as he dragged himself across the grass.

A doctor was consulted, of course. He diagnosed gallbladder trouble. A diet of raw fruits and vegetables was prescribed. Yet there was no improvement in Gehrig's condition.

In late April, the Yankees played the Senators, losing 3-1. Gehrig had a single in three at-bats. It was his 2,721st hit—and the final one of his career.

On May 2, Gehrig asked for a meeting with manager Joe McCarthy. "I'm benching myself, Joe," he said, as related in *Iron Horse*. "Why?" was the manager's hesitant response. "For the good of the team, Joe," Gehrig continued. "Nobody has to tell

Lou Gehrig put his arm around teammate Ellsworth "Babe" Dahlgren in the dugout on May 2, 1939, when the Yankees were playing at Detroit. Gehrig, who had become noticeably weaker in the past year, took himself out of the lineup and was replaced by Dahlgren. Gehrig's consecutive-game streak had ended—at 2,130 games.

me how bad I've been and how much of a drawback I've been to the club. I've been thinking ever since the season opened, when I couldn't start as I hoped I would, that the time has come for me to quit.

"I just don't know," Lou went on, his head hanging low. "I can't figure what's the matter with me. I just know I can't go on this way."

The Iron Horse, the Iron Man, the Yankee team captain, whose steadfast efforts and determination had made him a legend in his own time, limped away from baseball after 2,130 straight games.

The Pride
of the Yankees

The Mayo Clinic is today one of the leading medical research centers in the world. In 1939, it was essentially the only such facility of its kind. Founded by two brothers, doctors William and Charles Mayo, the Mayo Clinic pioneered group practice, in which the clinician, the specialist, and the laboratory worker pull together as a team for the patient's well-being. If Lou Gehrig was ever to find out what was sapping his strength, pulling him down, forcing him to retire from the game he loved, surely the Mayo Clinic would have the answer.

To the Mayo Clinic, therefore, Gehrig would go. It was the first week in June 1939, and he wanted, desperately, to determine finally what was destroying his body.

Before Gehrig departed, Eleanor had a request of Dr. Charles Mayo himself. "Do me a favor," she said to him in a private phone conversation, as recalled in *My Luke and I.* "When you make the diagnosis, call me—don't tell Lou."

"Are you sure?" Dr. Mayo asked Eleanor. "It's the policy of the Mayo Clinic to tell the facts to the head of the house."

Eleanor's response was swift and direct. "I've got news for you," she said. "*I'm* the head of the house."

Gehrig's arrival in Rochester, Minnesota, on June 13 was reported with crushing directness in Eleanor's autobiography:

> The first staff man who watched Lou's arrival at the Mayo Clinic was Dr. Harold C. Habein. It was the first time Dr. Habein had ever seen the celebrated captain of the New York Yankees. He shook hands, then said: "Excuse me a moment, Lou."

To Harold Habein, the impression was unmistakable and devastating. He had watched his own mother die slowly with the same shuffling gait. He went straight inside to Dr. Mayo's private office and said: "My God, the boy's got amyotrophic lateral sclerosis."

A BIRTHDAY TO FORGET

Amyotrophic lateral sclerosis (AY-my-uh-tro-fik LAH-tuh-rul skluh-RO-sis), or ALS, is a degenerative muscle disease for which there is no cure. "A" stands for without; "myo" means muscle; "trophic" says nourishment; "lateral" refers to side (of the spinal cord); and "sclerosis" signals hardening or scarring. Although only one in 50,000 people can expect to get ALS, once a firm diagnosis is made, it is a downward cycle, usually leading to death in an average of three years.

Over time, ALS causes motor neurons in the brain and the spinal cord to shrink and disappear. Muscles no longer receive signals to move, thus becoming smaller and weaker. The disease usually begins with muscle weakness in the arms and legs. Soon, a person begins to trip and fall. He, or she, begins to drop things. Then, speech is affected, sometimes accompanied by uncontrollable periods of laughing or crying. Eventually, eating and swallowing becomes difficult. Finally, breathing ceases.

There are, curiously, two factors associated with ALS that, depending on how they are viewed, can make the disease all the more bizarre and frightening. There is, fortunately, little or no pain. And, being a blessing or a curse, the mind stays alert: The parts of the brain that allow one to think, remember, and learn are not affected. Thankful as that is, such awareness has been described by at least one ALS patient as "like being present at your own funeral."

Eleanor Gehrig got the call on, of all days, Lou Gehrig's thirty-sixth birthday, June 19, 1939. "On the outside," Eleanor relates in her autobiography, "they told me on the telephone he had two and a half years to live."

Although Gehrig was told he had ALS, he was not, on his wife's orders, given the full, devastating prognosis. In a letter Gehrig wrote to his wife from the Mayo Clinic, as detailed in *My Luke and I*, he declared, in that confident, optimistic tone so characteristic of him:

> There is a 50-50 chance of keeping me as I am. I may need a cane in 10 to 15 years. Playing is out of the question and Paul [Dr. O'Leary] suggests a coaching job or job in the office or writing. I made him honestly assure me that it will not affect me mentally.

Gehrig went on to promise his wife that there was no danger of transmission. "If there were [and I made them doubly assure me] you certainly would never have been allowed within 100 feet of me."

The Yankees held Lou Gehrig Appreciation Day on July 4, 1939. Players from the 1927 Murderers' Row team were among those in attendance. Gehrig, who was diagnosed with amyotrophic lateral sclerosis, gave one of the most memorable speeches in sports history.

LOU GEHRIG APPRECIATION DAY

Confronting ALS is daunting, even for a man as disciplined and optimistic as Lou Gehrig. Dealing with the media attention surrounding his illness only added to Gehrig's burden.

The celebrations were quick in coming, beginning with an all-out Yankee-style Stadium bash scheduled for the nation's birthday, on July 4, 1939. Billed as Lou Gehrig Appreciation Day, the reclusive Iron Man moaned at the mere thought of it.

Edward Barrow, the Yankees' general manager, scheduled events to take place between a doubleheader with the Washington Senators, all the better to ensure a huge crowd. Players from the Yankees' 1927 Murderers' Row team would be there, including Earle Combs, Tony Lazzeri, and Everett Scott. And, of course, Babe Ruth would be on hand. Fiorello LaGuardia, the mayor of New York City, was expected to make a short speech. And gifts galore would be presented.

Ceremonies got under way as scheduled, with manager Joe McCarthy speaking briefly to the 62,000 assembled fans. Fighting back tears, he said, as reported in *Iron Horse*:

> Lou, what else can I say except that it was a sad day in the life of everyone who knew you when you came to my hotel room that day in Detroit and told me you were quitting as a ballplayer because you felt yourself a hindrance to the team. . . . My God, man, you were never that.

There followed the presentation of numerous gifts and trophies, with Gehrig standing silently, cap in hand, head bowed.

Finally, the chant, "We want Gehrig, We want Gehrig," arose from the throng, rising to a deafening climax.

Gehrig was extremely reluctant to acknowledge the crowd's request. Emotion had overtaken him, and he doubted he could address his admirers. Although Gehrig had prepared a speech the evening before, under the best of circumstances he was no public speaker. These were anything but the best of times.

Still, with no indication the chanting would let up, Gehrig approached the microphone. What was but an instant before a thunderous roar now descended into a deadening silence. Gehrig took a deep breath and started to speak, delivering what is considered to be the most memorable speech in sports history:

"Fans, for the past two weeks, you have been reading about a bad break I got," he began, his voice breaking, as narrated in *Iron Horse*. "Yet today I consider myself the luckiest man on the face of the earth."

Gehrig then proceeded slowly, somewhat haltingly, never looking up at the crowd:

> I have been in ballparks for seventeen years and I have never received anything but kindness and encouragement from you fans. Look at these grand men. Which of you wouldn't consider it the highlight of his career just to associate with them for even one day? Sure, I'm lucky. Who wouldn't consider it an honor to have known Jacob Ruppert? Also, the builder of baseball's greatest empire, Ed Barrow? To have spent six years with that wonderful little fellow, Miller Huggins? Then to have spent the next nine years with that outstanding leader, that smart student of psychology, the best manager in baseball today, Joe McCarthy? Sure, I'm lucky. When the New York Giants, a team you would give your right arm to beat, and vice versa, sends you a gift, that's something. When everybody down to the groundskeepers and those boys in white coats remember you with trophies, that's something. When you have a father and mother who work all their lives so that you can have an education and build your body, it's a blessing. When you have a wife who has been a tower of strength and shown more courage than you dreamed existed, that's the finest I know. So I close in saying that I might have had a bad break, but I have an awful lot to live for. Thank you.

A JOB TO DO

Gehrig, not yet ready to retire and waste away, was hoping for a position with the Yankees organization, perhaps as a coach, a scout, or in the front office. The offer never came.

New York City mayor Fiorello LaGuardia shook hands with Lou Gehrig after administering the oath of office to Gehrig as a new member of the city's parole commission. With them were Eleanor Gehrig and John C. Maher, a parole commissioner. Gehrig was able to work at the job for a year until his condition deteriorated too much.

The mayor did come through, however, and with a real, not a showcase, job. LaGuardia asked Gehrig to become one of his three parole commissioners. Gehrig accepted, even moving to live within the city limits as the law required one to do in such a position.

Though his physical condition continued to deteriorate, eventually to the point where Gehrig could barely hold a pen in his hand, he sat at his drab desk, day after day, listening to potential parolees tell him what a bad break they had received. Gehrig must have thought, "You talk about a bad break?" but he never let on. Eventually, the strain of being driven to the office every day was too much. A year after taking the commissioner's job, Gehrig resigned.

On December 7, 1939, the Baseball Writers' Association of America voted Gehrig into the Baseball Hall of Fame. At that time, no waiting period was required for induction, thus Gehrig lived to see the honor bestowed upon him.

Shortly thereafter, the Yankees did something no baseball team had ever done—they retired a player's number. From then on, no Yankee would ever wear a jersey with the number 4. That number was Lou Gehrig's and no other's.

Robbed of everything he had always cherished, Gehrig saw his physical condition worsen. He could not walk. His arms were useless. He could not light his pipe. When he played bridge, someone had to hold his cards. Toward the end, he could barely swallow a drink or utter a word.

That end came on June 2, 1941, while Gehrig lay sleeping in his bed. He was but 37 years old. From that time on, amyotrophic lateral sclerosis would also be known as Lou Gehrig's disease.

Gehrig's funeral took place on June 4, at Christ Church in New York City. It was a simple, dignified affair. At the request of the family, no eulogy was given. Yet, in her 1976 autobiography, Eleanor gave as fitting a tribute as one could when she said:

> I would not have traded two minutes of the joy and the grief with that man for two decades of anything with another. Happy or sad, filled with great expectations or great frustrations, we had attained it for whatever brief instant that fate had decided. The most in life, the unattainable, and we were not star-crossed by it. We were blessed with it, my Luke and I.

THE PRIDE OF THE YANKEES

In the fall of 1941, Hollywood film producer Samuel Gold-wyn was approached with the idea of doing a movie about Lou Gehrig's life. "If people want to see a baseball game, they should go to a ballpark" was his initial response, as reported in *Iron Horse*.

Goldwyn's dismissal of the film concept was not surprising, being that he knew so little about the game. Goldwyn thought there were 10 bases on a diamond. Later, when the producer found out that Gehrig had played first base, he bemoaned the

☆ ☆ ☆ ☆ ☆

NATIONAL BASEBALL HALL OF FAME

Babe Ruth, Ty Cobb, Walter Johnson, Christy Mathewson, and Honus Wagner were the first inductees of the then-newly formed National Baseball Hall of Fame in 1936. The Hall of Fame Museum opened three years later, in Cooperstown, New York. During the museum's opening ceremonies, Babe Ruth said:

"They started something here and the kids are keeping the ball rolling. I hope some of you kids will be in the Hall of Fame. I'm very glad that in my day I was able to earn my place. And I hope youngsters of today have the same opportunity to experience such feelings."

The Baseball Writers' Association of America (BBWAA) votes on who makes it into the National Baseball Hall of Fame. Each year, each writer may vote for as many as 10 candidates, or as few as zero. To qualify, a writer must have covered major-league baseball for at least 10 years.

There are five requirements, according to the National Baseball Hall of Fame Web site:

fact, suggesting that it would have been better to have at least played third or fourth.

Nonetheless, promoters were finally able to get Goldwyn into a studio screening room, where they could show him newsreel footage of Gehrig's July 4, 1939, farewell speech at Yankee Stadium. The lights dimmed. When they came back up, Goldwyn was sobbing uncontrollably. "Run it over again," he demanded. *The Pride of the Yankees* was soon on a fast track to reality.

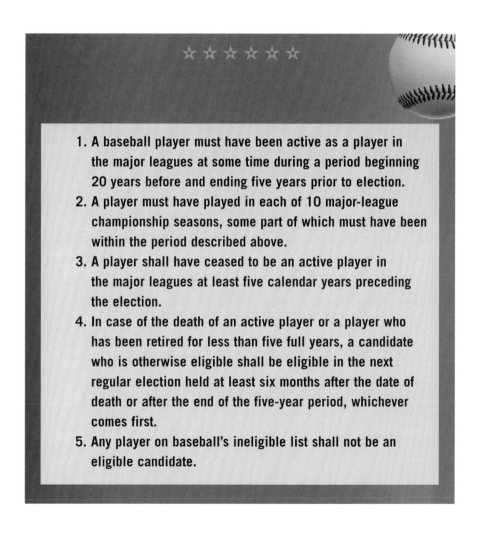

☆ ☆ ☆ ☆ ☆

1. A baseball player must have been active as a player in the major leagues at some time during a period beginning 20 years before and ending five years prior to election.
2. A player must have played in each of 10 major-league championship seasons, some part of which must have been within the period described above.
3. A player shall have ceased to be an active player in the major leagues at least five calendar years preceding the election.
4. In case of the death of an active player or a player who has been retired for less than five full years, a candidate who is otherwise eligible shall be eligible in the next regular election held at least six months after the date of death or after the end of the five-year period, whichever comes first.
5. Any player on baseball's ineligible list shall not be an eligible candidate.

Babe Ruth paused beside the body of Lou Gehrig during his funeral at Christ Church in New York City. Gehrig died on June 2, 1941, at age 37. The illness he suffered, amyotrophic lateral sclerosis, has come to be more commonly known as Lou Gehrig's disease.

The movie, starring Gary Cooper, was released in early 1942. It was an instant success, garnering 11 Academy Award nominations, including Best Picture.

The Pride of the Yankees was no documentary. It got dates and places mixed up, and took liberties with the facts, as Hollywood felt free to do. Still, it was a film faithful to Lou Gehrig's life and legacy. A man steady and true, who simply went out and did the job he loved every day—play baseball.

STATISTICS

LOU GEHRIG
Primary position: First base

Full name: Henry Louis Gehrig
- Born: June 19, 1903, New York, NY
- Died: June 2, 1941, Riverdale, NY
- Height: 6'0" • Weight: 200 lbs.
- Team: New York Yankees (1923–1939)

☆☆☆☆☆

YEAR	TEAM	G	AB	H	HR	RBI	BA
1923	NYY	13	26	11	1	9	.423
1924	NYY	10	12	6	0	5	.500
1925	NYY	126	437	129	20	68	.295
1926	NYY	155	572	179	16	112	.313
1927	NYY	155	584	218	47	175	.373
1928	NYY	154	562	210	27	142	.374
1929	NYY	154	553	166	35	126	.300
1930	NYY	154	581	220	41	174	.379
1931	NYY	155	619	211	46	184	.341
1932	NYY	156	596	208	34	151	.349
1933	NYY	152	593	198	32	139	.334
1934	NYY	154	579	210	49	165	.363
1935	NYY	149	535	176	30	119	.329
1936	NYY	155	579	205	49	152	.354
1937	NYY	157	569	200	37	159	.351
1938	NYY	157	576	170	29	114	.295
1939	NYY	8	28	4	0	1	.143
TOTALS		2,164	8,001	2,721	493	1,995	.340

Key: NYY = New York Yankees; G = Games; AB = At-bats; H = Hits; HR = Home runs;
RBI = Runs batted in; BA = Batting average

CHRONOLOGY

1903   **June 19** Born in New York City.

1917   Graduates from Public School 132 (eighth grade), with perfect attendance.

1920   **June 26** Hits grand slam for High School of Commerce at Wrigley Field.

1921   **January 27** Graduates from High School of Commerce.

        Fall Enters Columbia University on a football scholarship.

1923   **April 30** Signs first contract with Yankees.

        June 11 First arrives at Yankee Stadium.

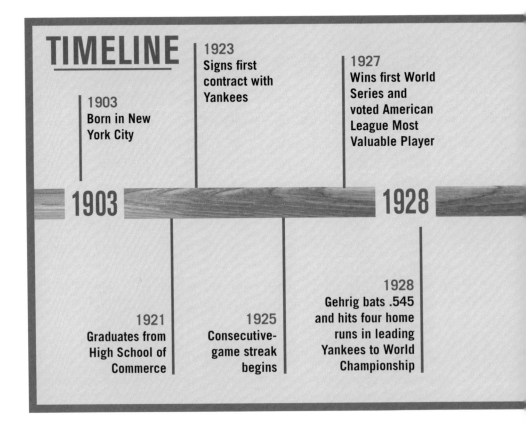

TIMELINE

1923
Signs first contract with Yankees

1927
Wins first World Series and voted American League Most Valuable Player

1903
Born in New York City

1903

1928

1921
Graduates from High School of Commerce

1925
Consecutive-game streak begins

1928
Gehrig bats .545 and hits four home runs in leading Yankees to World Championship

1924   Spends season playing in minor leagues; hits .369 with 37 home runs.

1925   **June 1** Pinch-hits and begins his consecutive-game streak.

1926   Plays in his first World Series; the Yankees fall to the St. Louis Cardinals in the Fall Classic.

1927   Vies with Babe Ruth during most of the season for the league lead in home runs; Gehrig finishes with 47, Ruth with 60; wins first World Series; voted the American League Most Valuable Player.

1928   Yankees again win World Series; Gehrig bats .545 and hits four home runs in the four-game sweep of the St. Louis Cardinals.

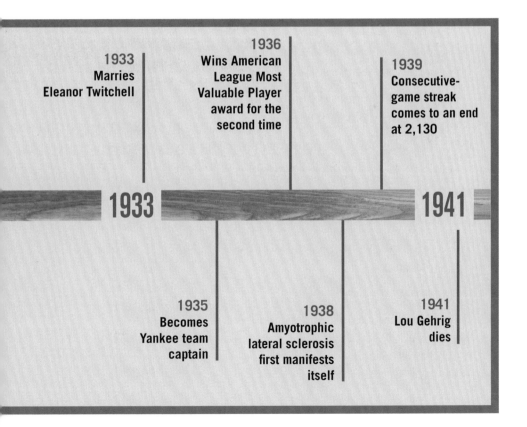

1933 Marries Eleanor Twitchell

1936 Wins American League Most Valuable Player award for the second time

1939 Consecutive-game streak comes to an end at 2,130

1933   **1941**

1935 Becomes Yankee team captain

1938 Amyotrophic lateral sclerosis first manifests itself

1941 Lou Gehrig dies

1931   Gehrig meets Eleanor Twitchell at a party, falls in love.

1932   **June 3** Hits four home runs in a single game; Yankees sweep Cubs in the World Series.

1933   **September 29** Lou and Eleanor are married.

1934   Is knocked unconscious when hit by a pitch during a mid-season exhibition game; wins Triple Crown for leading the American League in home runs, RBIs, and batting average.

1935   **April 12** Becomes Yankee team captain.

1936   Wins American League Most Valuable Player award for the second time; Yankees defeat the New York Giants in the World Series.

1937   Makes the movie *Rawhide*.

1938   Amyotrophic lateral sclerosis (ALS) first manifests itself.

   May 31 Eleanor asks Lou to stop his consecutive-game streak at 1,999 games.

1939   **May 2** Removes himself from Yankee lineup, having played 2,130 consecutive games.

   June 13 Visits Mayo Clinic.

   June 19 Eleanor is told Lou has ALS.

   July 4 Lou Gehrig Appreciation Day at Yankee Stadium.

1941   **June 2** Lou Gehrig dies.

1942   The film *The Pride of the Yankees* is released.

GLOSSARY

amyotrophic lateral sclerosis (ALS)   An incurable disease in which degeneration of motor neurons in the brain stem and spinal cord leads to atrophy and eventually complete paralysis of the voluntary muscles.

at-bat (AB)   An official turn at batting that is charged to a baseball player, except when the player walks, sacrifices, is hit by a pitched ball, or is interfered with by a catcher. At-bats are used to calculate a player's batting average and slugging percentage.

base on balls   The awarding of first base to a batter after a pitcher throws four balls. Also known as a walk, it is "intentional" when the four balls are thrown on purpose to avoid pitching to a batter.

batter's box   The area to the left and right of home plate in which the batter must be standing for fair play to take place.

batting average   The number of hits a batter gets divided by the number of times the player is at bat. For example, 3 hits in 10 at-bats would be a .300 batting average.

beanball   The act of the pitcher hitting the batter with the pitch.

bottom of the inning   The second half of an inning, during which the home team bats.

brushback   A pitch intentionally thrown close to a batter (especially when he is crowding the plate) to "brush him back."

bunt   A ball not fully hit, with the batter either intending to get to first base before the infielder can field the ball, or allowing an existing base runner to advance a base.

cleanup hitter   The fourth batter in the lineup, usually a power hitter. The team hopes runners are on base for the "cleanup" hitter to drive home.

curveball   A pitch that curves on its way to the plate, thanks to the spin a pitcher places on the ball when throwing. Also know as a "breaking ball."

Dead Ball Era   The time period before the Live Ball Era, when the structure of the baseball did not have the liveliness it has today. Most historians agree that the Dead Ball Era ended after the 1919 season.

doubleheader   Two games played by the same two teams on the same day.

earned run   A run that is made without an error, passed ball, or catcher's interference.

earned-run average (ERA)   A statistic that indicates the number of earned runs a pitcher gives up (on average) in a nine-inning game.

error   The game's scorer designates an error when a defensive player makes a mistake that results in a runner reaching or advancing to a base.

fastball   A ball thrown at a high velocity by the pitcher. Many of today's major-league pitchers can throw more than 90 miles per hour (145 kilometers per hour).

games behind   A statistic used in team standings. It is figured by adding the difference in wins between a trailing team and the leader to the difference in losses, and dividing by two. So a team that is three games behind may trail by three in the win column and three in the loss column, or four and two, or any other combination of wins and losses totaling six.

grand slam   An event that occurs when the batter hits a home run with the bases loaded.

home run   When a batter hits a ball into the stands in fair territory, it is a home run. The batter may also have an inside-the-park home run if the ball never leaves the playing field and the runner is able to reach home plate without stopping before being tagged by a defensive player. A home run counts as one run, and if there are any runners on base when a home run is hit, they too score.

lineup A list that is presented to the umpire and opposing manager before the start of the game that contains the order in which the batters will bat as well as the defensive fielding positions they will play.

Live Ball Era The period beginning after the 1919 season when the construction of the baseball improved significantly, with a cork center and a tighter-wound yarn that made the ball "livelier."

on-base percentage The number of times a player reaches base divided by the number of plate appearances.

on deck The player that is scheduled to bat after the current batter is referred to as being "on deck." He is required to stand in the on-deck circle that is reserved for practice swings.

runs batted in (RBI) The number of runs that score as a direct result of a batter's hit(s) are the runs batted in by that batter.

sacrifice A ball hit by the batter that advances the runner to the next base while the batter receives an "out" for his attempt. Examples include a sacrifice fly and a sacrifice bunt.

screwball A pitch that curves to the same side as it was thrown from. For a right-handed pitcher, the ball would break to his right—"in" to a right-handed hitter. Also known as a reverse curve or a fadeaway.

slider A relatively fast pitch with a slight curve in the opposite direction of the throwing arm.

slugging percentage   The number of bases a player reaches divided by the number of at-bats. It is a measure of the power of a batter.

strike zone   The area above home plate that extends from midway between a batter's shoulders and his belt to an area just below the kneecap. Through time, the strike zone has changed, and even today, relies on the judgment of the umpire.

top of the inning   The first half of an inning during which the away team bats.

Triple Crown   A player wins the Triple Crown when he leads the league in batting average, home runs, and runs batted in at the end of a season.

wild pitch   A pitcher is charged with a wild pitch when, according to the official scorer, a pitch is too high, too low, or too wide for the catcher to catch the ball with ordinary effort, and when that pitch also allows one or more runners to advance.

BIBLIOGRAPHY

BOOKS

Angell, Roger. *Game Time: A Baseball Companion.* New York: Harvest Book/Harcourt, Inc., 2003.

Asinof, Eliot. *Eight Men Out: The Black Sox and the 1919 World Series.* New York: Henry Holt and Company, 1963.

Banks, Kerry. *The Babe Ruth Era: Old-Time Baseball Trivia.* Vancouver/Toronto: Greystone Books, 1998.

Deford, Frank. *The Old Ball Game: How John McGraw, Christy Mathewson, and the New York Giants Created Modern Baseball.* New York: Atlantic Monthly Press, 2005.

DiMaggio, Joe. *Lucky to Be a Yankee.* New York: Grosset & Dunlap, 1951.

Eig, Jonathan. *Luckiest Man: The Life and Death of Lou Gehrig.* New York: Simon & Schuster, 2005.

Gehrig, Eleanor, and Joseph Durso. *My Luke and I.* New York: New American Library, 1976.

Gillette, Gary, and Peter Palmer. *The 2006 ESPN Baseball Encyclopedia.* New York: Sterling Publishing Co., Inc., 2006.

Graham, Frank. *The New York Yankees: An Informal History.* Carbondale and Edwardsville, Ill.: Southern Illinois University Press, 1943.

Halberstam, David. *Summer of '49.* New York: Harper Perennial Modern Classics, 1989.

Kennedy, Kevin, with Bill Gutman. *Twice Around the Bases: The Thinking Fan's Inside Look at Baseball.* New York: Harper, 2005.

Montville, Leigh. *The Big Bam: The Life and Times of Babe Ruth.* New York: Doubleday, 2006.

Nemec, David, and Scott Flatow. *Great Baseball Feats, Facts & Firsts.* New York: Signet, 2006.

Robinson, Ray. *Iron Horse: Lou Gehrig in His Time.* New York: W.W. Norton & Company, 1990.

Stout, Glenn. *Yankee Century: 100 Years of New York Yankee Baseball.* Boston: Houghton Mifflin, 2002.

NEWSPAPERS

Dawson, James. "Gehrig's Four Hits Help Yankees Win." *New York Times*, May 11, 1934.

———. "Ruth's Record of 700 Home Runs Likely to Stand for All Time in Major Leagues." *New York Times*, July 14, 1934.

———. "Gehrig Voluntarily Ends Streak at 2,130 Straight Games." *New York Times*, May 3, 1939.

———. "McCarthy at Fair, Deftly Parries Vexing Query Posed by Youngster." *New York Times*, May 16, 1939.

———. "Gehrig Reported Ailing." *New York Times*, June 2, 1939.

———. "Yanks Never to Use Gehrig's 'No. 4' Again; Veteran Put on Retired List, Not Released." *New York Times*, January 7, 1940.

———. "Funeral Service for Gehrig Is Held." *New York Times*, June 5, 1941.

Dunlap, Orrin. "Ceremony Is Carried by Television as Industry Makes Its Formal Bow." *New York Times*, May 1, 1939.

———. "Buoyant Gehrig, Long String Ended, Puzzled Over His Batting Decline." *New York Times*, May 4, 1939.

Harrison, James. "Yanks Sweep Series, Wild Pitch Beating Pirates, 4-3, in Ninth." *New York Times*, October 9, 1927.

———. "Boys Jam Trenton Field and Stop Game When Ruth Hits His Third Homer of Day." *New York Times*, October 11, 1927.

Kieran, John. "Sports of the Times." *New York Times,* October 26, 1927.

———. "Ruth, Gehrig Back; Played in 9 States." *New York Times,* November 9, 1927.

McGowen, Roscoe. "Gehrig, Back, Hopes to Eclipse Ruth." *New York Times,* February 14, 1935.

———. "Equinoctial Climax." *Time,* October 5, 1936.

———. "Gehrig Seeks Role as Tarzan in Films." *New York Times,* October 21, 1936.

———. "Gehrig Sets Goal at 2,500 Straight." *New York Times,* January 31, 1937.

———. "Gehrig Signs for Movies, Bars Tarzan Role; Says He Has No Idea of Quitting Baseball." *New York Times,* March 4, 1937.

———. "Gehrig, the 'Iron Man' of Baseball, Now Looks Ahead to 2,500 Games." *New York Times,* June 1, 1938.

———. "Letter to the Sports Editor: Much Ado About Lou." *New York Times,* October 8, 1938.

Vidmer, Richards. "Fans Worship Ruth But Forget Gehrig." *New York Times,* July 20, 1927.

———. "Yanks Are Stopped, But Only by Rain." *New York Times,* August 1, 1927.

———. "Yanks Make Sweep of Detroit Series." *New York Times,* August 27, 1927.

FILM

Goldwyn, Samuel. *The Pride of the Yankees.* Metro Goldwyn Mayer, 1942.

WEB SITES

ALS Association
http://www.alsa.org/

Baseball Almanac
http://www.baseball-almanac.com/

Baseball Links
http://www.baseball-links.com/

Heavyhitter.com
http://www.heavyhitter.com/

Historic Baseball
http://www.historicbaseball.com/

Kid's Health: Lou Gehrig Disease
http://kidshealth.org/kid/grownup/conditions/als.html

Lou Gehrig: The Official Web Site
http://www.lougehrig.com/

National Baseball Hall of Fame and Museum
http://www.baseballhalloffame.org/

Official Site of Major League Baseball
http://mlb.mlb.com/index.jsp

Official Site of the New York Yankees
http://www.yankees.com

FURTHER READING

Abramovitz, Melissa. *Diseases and Disorders: Lou Gehrig's Disease.* Farmington Hills, Mich.: Lucent Books, 2006.

Adler, David. *Lou Gehrig: The Luckiest Man.* New York: Voyager Books/Harcourt, Inc., 1997.

Bak, Richard. *Lou Gehrig: An American Classic.* Lanham, Md.: Taylor Trade Publishing, 1995.

Buckley Jr., James. *Classic Ballparks.* New York: Barnes & Noble Books, 2004.

Burleigh, Robert. *Home Run: The Story of Babe Ruth.* New York: Voyager Books/Harcourt, Inc., 1998.

Christopher, Matt. *Great Moments in Baseball History.* New York: Little, Brown, 1996.

Karpin, Howie. *Yankees Essential: Everything You Need to Know to Be a Real Fan.* Chicago: Triumph Books, 2007.

MacKay, Claire. *Touching All the Bases: Baseball for Kids of All Ages.* Tonawanda, N.Y.: Firefly Books Ltd., 1996.

Mintzer, Rich. *The Everything Kids' Baseball Book.* Cincinnati: Adams Media Group, 2004.

Morgan, Joe. *Baseball for Dummies.* Hoboken, N.J.: Wiley Publishing, Inc., 2005.

Van Riper, Guernsey. *Lou Gehrig: One of Baseball's Greatest.* New York: Aladdin Paperbacks, 1986.

Viola, Kevin. *Lou Gehrig.* Minneapolis: Lerner Publications Company, 2005.

WEB SITES

Baseball Reference
http://www.baseball-reference.com

"Gehrig's Shining Legacy of Courage"
http://mlb.mlb.com/nyy/history/gehrig.jsp

Lou Gehrig: Farewell to Baseball Address
http://www.americanrhetoric.com/speeches/lougehrigfarewelltobaseball.htm

PICTURE CREDITS

INDEX

ABOUT THE AUTHOR

RONALD A. REIS is the author of 13 books, including young adult biographies of Eugenie Clark and Jonas Salk. He is the chairman of the technology department at Los Angeles Valley College.